FOSTER CARE SOLUTIONS

PRACTICAL TOOLS FOR

# FOSTER PARENTS

Editors

LANA TEMPLE-PLOTZ, M.S.

TED P. STRICKLETT, M.S.

CHRISTENA B. BAKER, M.S.W.

MICHAEL N. STERBA, M.H.D.

Based on Girls and Boys Town's
Common Sense Parenting®

BOYS
TOWN
PRESS

BOYS TOWN, NEBRASKA

# Practical Tools for Foster Parents

Published by the Boys Town Press
Father Flanagan's Boys' Home
Boys Town, NE 68010

Copyright © 2002 by Father Flanagan's Boys' Home

ISBN 978-1-889322-49-0

The Boys Town Press is the publishing division of Girls and Boys Town, the original Father Flanagan's Boys' Home.

### Publisher's Cataloging-in-Publication
#### (Provided by Quality Books, Inc.)

Practical tools for foster parents / editors, Lana
   Temple-Plotz ... [et al.]. -- 1st ed.
      p. cm.
      Includes bibliographical references and index.
      ISBN: 978-1-889322-49-0

   1. Foster parents--United States--Handbooks, manuals, etc. 2. Foster home care--United States--Handbooks, manuals, etc. I. Temple-Plotz, Lana.

HQ759.7.P73 2001                    362.73'3
                                    QBI01-200812

10   9   8   7   6   5   4   3

# PRACTICAL TOOLS FOR
# FOSTER PARENTS

## Also from the Boys Town Press

*Common Sense Parenting*®
*Common Sense Parenting of Toddlers and Preschoolers*
*Common Sense Parenting Learn-at-Home Video Kit*
*No Room for Bullies*
*Changing Children's Behavior by Changing the*
   *People, Places, and Activities in Their Lives*
*Who's Raising Your Child?*
*There Are No Simple Rules for Dating My Daughter*
*Good Night, Sweet Dreams, I Love You,*
   *Now Get into Bed and Go to Sleep*
*Tools for Teaching Social Skills in School*
*Angry Kids, Frustrated Parents*
*Dealing with Your Kids' 7 Biggest Troubles*
*Parenting to Build Character in Your Teen*
*Rebuilding Children's Lives*
*Skills for Families, Skills for Life*
*Building Skills in High-Risk Families*
*Dangerous Kids*
*Safe and Effective Secondary Schools*
*Teaching Social Skills to Youth*
*The Well-Managed Classroom*
*Unmasking Sexual Con Games*

## For Adolescents

*Boundaries: A Guide for Teens*
*A Good Friend*
*Who's in the Mirror?*
*What's Right for Me?*
*Little Sisters, Listen Up!*
*Guys, Let's Keep It Real!*

**For a Boys Town Press catalog, call 1-800-282-6657.**
**www.boystownpress.org**

# Girls and Boys Town National Hotline
# 1-800-448-3000

**Parents can call the Girls and Boys Town**
**National Hotline with any problem at any time.**

# Table of Contents

to this book: Father Val J. Peter, Executive Director; Jerry Davis, Associate Executive Director of Program and Staff Development; Kim Culp; Director of Support Services for Program and Staff Development; Ron Herron, Director of the Writing Division; Terry Hyland, Senior Writer/Editor of the Writing Division; Liz Gauger, Senior Writer/Editor of the Writing Division; and Lynn Holm, Editor for the Boys Town Press.

A special thanks goes to the following Girls and Boys Town Review Team members for their reviews and recommendations: Karen Authier, Paula Jones, Julie Nickolisen, Bobbie O'Connor, Pauline Patrick, Julie Swain, and Cindy Tierney.

Finally, our heartfelt gratitude and admiration to all the Foster Parents, kinship providers, case managers, and administrators who strive every day to create safe and happy homes for the foster children in their care.

# Acknowledgments

This book is based on information contained in the following books published by the Boys Town Press: *Common Sense Parenting* (Authors: Ray Burke, Ph.D. & Ron Herron), *Issues in Quality Child Care: A Boys Town Perspective* (Editors: Tom Dowd, Ron Herron, Terry Hyland, & Michael Sterba), and *Rebuilding Children's Lives* (Authors: Christena Baker, Ray Burke, Ron Herron, & Mariam Mott). Content was adapted to this book in order to address the specific needs of traditional Foster Parents who care for kids in their homes.

A tremendous thanks goes to all Girls and Boys Town Foster Family Service staff, past and present, who have contributed to the development of the ideas and content we share on the following pages. Too numerous to mention individually, their personal contributions have laid the foundation for the Girls and Boys Town Foster Family Service program.

We also would like to thank the following Girls and Boys Town administrators and staff for their contributions

# Foster Care: Making a Difference for America's Children

It's not easy being a kid these days. The world has become a very complicated place. Many children and adolescents are suffering the harmful effects of damaging forces that sweep across society and redefine our culture – soaring divorce rates and the slow breakdown of the traditional family, everyday aggression and violence rooted in disrespect, an eroding sense of connectedness to others, the age-old gap between wealth and poverty, and others.

The world today is even more frightening for young people because they don't have the authority or perspective to change these forces on their own. When a child's world crumbles around him or her, a helping hand is needed. You can be that helping hand; you can be that person who safely guides children and adolescents through troubled, turbulent times. How? With the love and compassion you already possess, combined with the practical suggestions and effective methods developed by the Girls and Boys Town foster care program.

Girls and Boys Town has a long history of success. More than 80 years after our founder, Father Edward Flanagan, took in five boys who were poor and had nowhere to go, the world-famous organization continues to reach out to boys, girls, and families who are in trouble. Over the years, we have developed a model of care – the Girls and Boys Town Teaching Model – and refined, adapted, and nurtured it through experience and research in order to help thousands of children and families every day. Today, Girls and Boys Town is a national leader in child care.

> **When a child's world crumbles around him or her, a helping hand is needed.**

As a Foster Parent, you will be on the front lines of the battle to help make children's lives better. There will be good times and bad times. It won't be easy. As a matter of fact, being a Foster Parent may be one of the most challenging jobs you'll ever have. But the children need you!

According to studies, the number of children removed from their families by the child welfare system continues to grow. During the 1980s, an estimated 260,000 children were in out-of-home care. By 1997, that figure had increased to more than 500,000. And more of these children had special needs (Annie E. Casey Foundation, 2000).

It's painful to realize that destructive forces like abuse and neglect, poverty, drug and alcohol abuse, and unemployment continue to take their toll on American children and families. And, as the problems and numbers of at-risk children and families increase, society becomes less able to respond to the greater need. Gaze beyond the statistics and you'll see the many faces of children in foster care.

But the news is not all bad; there is hope! Each day, caring people like you make a commitment to girls and boys in their communities by becoming Foster Parents. These individuals, who open their hearts and homes to troubled children, are richly rewarded through the satisfaction of knowing they have touched and changed lives. And the kids they care for find safety, genuine caring, and the opportunity to learn new skills.

Father Flanagan believed in the power of love and teaching to help kids find their way in the world. He charged all those who work with children to care deeply and never give up. *"Often it has been said that youth is the nation's greatest asset,"* Father Flanagan said. *"But it is more than that – it is the world's greatest asset. More than that, it is perhaps the world's only hope."*

This book is not about child development and complicated theories on why kids do what they do. Rather, it's a look at Girls and Boys Town's approach to foster care for the 21st century, which focuses on teaching skills, building relationships, and empowering kids through teaching them self-discipline and self-control. This approach is based on the belief that we have an obligation to build a brighter future for our children. The Girls and Boys Town Teaching Model helps Foster Parents learn how to provide a safe home for kids, and how to deal with their behaviors

– both positive and negative. You already possess many strengths and skills as a Foster Parent. Our hope is to help you improve your existing skills and strengths, and develop new ones.

Whether you're an experienced Foster Parent, a new Foster Parent, or a relative who's taken in a young family member during a difficult time, you can benefit from the practical advice and straightforward methods offered here. We welcome and admire your commitment to help bring healing and hope, through love and guidance, to troubled children and adolescents at a time when they need it most.

# CHAPTER 1

# Building a Relationship with Your Foster Child

*Tom walked into the kitchen where Chris, his foster mother, was preparing dinner.*

*"Look who's here!" said Chris. "The best basketball player around! Congratulations on making the varsity Tom. I'm making spaghetti. Your brother said we should have something special for dinner to celebrate."*

*"Thanks Chris. I am so jazzed! This could mean I get a scholarship!" Tom said, smiling.*

*"Maybe. You worked hard this year and you deserved to make the varsity! Do you want to play pro ball someday?"*

*"Absolutely," said Tom. "Maybe with the Lakers, if they'd have me."*

*"They'd be lucky to get you! Would you mind helping me get the table set so we can get everybody in here for dinner and hear about your day?"*

*"Sure."*

*"Thanks, Tom. Whew! We haven't had this kind of excitement around here in a long time. I've never had a meal with a future NBA player before!" Chris said.*
*"Trust me, you'll do fine," Tom said with a laugh.*

Taking the time to build relationships with the children in your care is an important part of your job as a Foster Parent. And as you can see from the example, making that connection with foster children can be as simple as using praise and talking with them every day.

Many children in foster care have not yet learned how to develop positive relationships. Others misuse what they have learned, and some simply don't understand how it's done. It might not be easy for them to make and keep friends. They might have problems getting along with adults in authority (parents, teachers, employers, and others), and they also might have trouble forming attachments to those that care for them.

Developing and nurturing relationships is an essential key to living a rewarding and happy life. Young people who have not learned these necessary skills are missing the friendship and love they need from others as they grow. That is why building positive relationships with children in your care is so critical. Not only are you teaching them how to develop healthy relationships with others, but you also are creating an atmosphere of trust and security between yourself and your foster child. This will help you in your teaching and make it more likely that youngsters will benefit from their experiences in foster care. And per-

haps more importantly, it helps children develop a positive set of values that they can use forever, and in any situation, as a basis for making their own decisions.

## Why Kids Can't Connect

As we've said, many children in foster care have a difficult time connecting with others in positive ways. Their relationships with parents, teachers, neighbors, and even friends may be characterized by apathy, defiance, dishonesty, and aggression. Some foster children have learned these behaviors from the adults in their lives, who, for a variety of reasons, have failed to be good role models. Or, young people may have developed these behaviors on their own, as a way to cope and survive in a difficult world. Whatever the reasons, these children must first learn how to trust and connect (or attach) with others before they can begin developing and building healthy relationships – and reaping the benefits that come from them.

### Attachment

Two respected researchers and authors on the subject of attachment, Marshall Klaus and John Kennell (1976), have defined attachment "as an affectionate bond between two individuals that endures through space and time and serves to join them emotionally." By the time most children enter foster care, they have been separated from many of the people with whom they have built relationships: parents, stepparents, relatives, babysitters, neighbors, friends, and others. In addition, these same children may have lived in

other settings like shelters, hospitals, or other foster homes. These children are at the greatest risk of having attachment problems because they worry about whom to trust to care for them.

What's important for Foster Parents to understand is that children who do not develop a secure primary attachment relationship (with mom, dad, grandparent, or another caregiver) are more likely to have problems with relationships, and these problems are likely to get worse when they enter foster care. The foster child who has been moved many times will have greater problems developing trusting relationships. Child welfare professionals used to think it was best to move a child from a stable foster care home so that the child wouldn't "get too close" to the foster family. We now know that this attachment, in fact, is necessary and should be encouraged with any caregiver who provides the right nurturing environment for the child.

**Developing and nurturing relationships is an essential key to living a rewarding and happy life.**

One of your toughest challenges as a Foster Parent is to accept the reality that, even though you may give foster children an abundance of kindness, care, and love, it's likely that they will not respond to you in the same manner all of the time. Because of this, you might begin to feel frustrated, view yourself as a "bad" Foster Parent, or even want to reject the child. Don't despair! These are normal feelings

that most Foster Parents feel at some time when children don't show gratitude and appreciation for all that you are doing for them. Our experience has taught us that when Foster Parents understand that these kinds of reactions are typical and not any fault of their own, it is much easier to not take a foster child's rejections personally.

What can you do when faced with this kind of situation? The best answer is to "stay the course." This means you should continue to build relationships, use the teaching tools described in this book, and remain consistent with consequences. A word of caution: Don't focus on these factors to the extent that you neglect or forget to show your foster child affection and how much you really care about him or her. Doing this will only damage a relationship. Balance is the key here. Unfortunately, you might not see the fruits of your labor while a child is in your care. By doing the things discussed here, you are planting a seed that might help the child learn to trust and attach to others later in life – whether that's at home with his or her family or with someone else in another placement.

## Importance of Attachment

All of us need to know that someone cares about us and loves us, and that others can be trusted to help us with problems that arise in life. This is especially true with children in foster care. According to Vera Fahlberg (1991), another author who has worked with hundreds of foster children, having a strong attachment with a caregiver allows children to develop trust in others and, ultimately, in themselves. They begin to have confidence that the world is a safe place where they can explore and have their basic needs met. These early relationships influence the child's physical and intellectual development and form the foundation for his or her psychological development. The child's earliest attachments become the example or blueprint for future relationships. When a responsive caregiver consistently meets a child's needs, it strengthens the development of secure attachments and a child's sense of relating to others.

The benefits of strong, healthy attachments for children are many. According to Fahlberg, children who develop these kinds of attachments are more likely to:

- Attain full intellectual potential.
- Sort out perceptions.
- Think logically.
- Develop social emotions.
- Develop a conscience.
- Trust others.
- Be resilient.
- Become self-reliant.
- Cope better with stress and frustration.
- Reduce feelings of jealousy.
- Overcome common fears and worries.
- Have increased feelings of self-worth.

One of the difficult realities about being a Foster Parent is that if you do your job well, your foster child will probably leave your home for a more permanent family. (Although, today, more Foster Parents are adopting foster children than ever before.) But just as you have created a safe environment that helped the child develop an attachment, you also can help that child learn that it is safe to leave and connect to other people. You have helped the child establish a strong foundation. Children may be concerned about being disloyal to you as they start to develop stronger attachments to their own parents or to a new permanent parent. That is why **they need clear messages and ongoing teaching from you about the benefits of caring for many people instead of only one.**

## Warning Signs of Attachment Problems

On the other hand, if a child's basic needs have not been met, or have been met in a very inconsistent manner, it can lead to attachment problems. The child may conclude that he or she cannot depend on others to meet his or her needs.

The following is a list of some warning signs that may indicate your foster child has an attachment problem. Some behaviors to be aware of include:

- Displaying superficially engaging and charming behaviors – they may "fake" their affection.
- Being overly affectionate with strangers.
- Showing developmental lags – the child may be interested in games or toys that much younger children like, or they may have tantrums like younger children do.
- Avoiding eye contact.

- Destroying own and/or others' belongings.
- Being uncomfortable with physical touch.
- Exhibiting cruelty toward siblings, foster brothers or sisters, or classmates.
- Being cruel toward animals.
- Having problems developing friendships with other children.
- Lacking "cause and effect" thinking – they don't understand the consequences of their behavior. They usually think it is someone else's fault.
- Overly clinging or demanding of your attention.
- Hoarding or gorging food.
- Fighting to control every aspect of the environment.
- Stealing and lying behaviors.
- Showing no remorse for negative behaviors.
- Having poor impulse control – they have trouble resisting the urge to do whatever comes to their minds.

## Developing Healthy Attachments

You have two tasks in this area when a foster child enters your home. The first task is to help the child develop a healthy attachment with you so that continued growth and development can occur. The second task is to help the child build on the attachments that he or she has already developed. That way, the improvements the child has achieved in your care can be carried over to future care-givers (birth parents, adoptive parents, or new Foster Parents).

The first step in the process of building healthy attachments is to help your foster child adjust to your home. Some suggestions for doing this are:

**Be honest about the placement.**

With the help of the caseworker, tell your foster child as much as you can about why he or she was placed in your home. Remember to take into account the child's age and ability to understand family problems.

**Be sure the child arrives with some personal possessions.**

This helps lessen the trauma of moving from a familiar home to an unfamiliar home. If your foster child arrives without any familiar possessions, talk together about some of his or her "favorite things" (stuffed animals, blanket, toys). Purchasing one of these items may help your foster child feel more secure in your home and will help to build your relationship with him or her.

**Keep your foster child active.**

Plan family activities and outings with the child.

**Be consistent.**

Set up clear house rules, routines, and expectations. This structure will enable your foster child to feel more "in control" because he or she will know what's expected instead of being told each time.

**Be supportive and empathetic.**

Provide your foster child with opportunities to express his or her grief through artwork, journaling, and discussion. Be understanding and keep in mind that the child needs time to heal.

**Praise! Praise! Praise!**

Find even small behaviors to praise – compliment and show approval verbally and nonverbally.

Linda Bayless and Lillie Love of the Child Welfare Institute (1990) have developed other ways Foster Parents can help a child adjust to a new home and begin to build healthy attachments. Some of these are:

**Identify activities and behaviors that represent your family, and include your foster child in them.**

For example, if each member of your family has a special place at the table and in the family room, then help the foster child to feel like part of your family by giving him or her one, too.

**Identify something each parent can do every day with the child for 15 minutes that will be pleasurable for the child and parent.**

This activity may be reading together, talking quietly about the day, or watching television. The key is that it should be enjoyable for you and the child.

**Identify a special role and responsibility for the child in your family.**

This can be something as simple as assisting with setting the table, helping to feed pets, and so on.

**Help the child to have mementos and memories of all significant people.**

Work with the child's family and caseworker to gather photographs, special toys, and keepsakes.

**Help children talk about their families.**

Encourage your foster child to talk about his or her family (activities they did together, trips, family traditions, etc.).

**Help children express feelings of loss or missing their families.**

Be open with your foster child about the times when you've felt a loss and encourage the child to express grief and sadness through journaling, writing letters, and other ways that help to overcome these feelings. Tell the child it's okay to feel this way, but unhealthy to dwell on it.

**Identify non-harmful ways the child can express anger, frustration, or sadness.**

We'll talk more in Chapter 16 about Teaching Self-Control, how to teach your foster child to express anger appropriately through developing a "Staying Calm Plan."

**Help children to remain connected to and have contact with significant people from their past.**

This may include parents, grandparents, siblings, or former Foster Parents. Talk with your foster child's caseworker to identify appropriate modes of communication (personal visits, phone contact, letter writing, etc.).

**Identify familiar and pleasurable things from the child's past and incorporate those things into your home.**

These can be things like special holiday traditions, ethnic foods, or favorite activities.

**Contact the Foster Care agency you are working for to seek professional help for the foster child when needed.**
If you feel overwhelmed or believe that your foster child has a severe problem, notify your caseworker. He or she may contact a professional (psychiatrist, psychologist, therapist, or other mental health provider) for help.

# Boundaries

Children in your care also may have difficulty identifying and setting proper boundaries. They may make poor choices about friends, perhaps trusting people they shouldn't trust or distancing themselves from others who may be good influences. That is why, many times, the most serious problems foster kids bring with them involve poor boundaries and sexual activity. These sexual issues can be unhealthy and extremely hazardous for all children. Besides the physical risk of pregnancy and sexually transmitted diseases, there's also the risk of further emotional pain and the possibility of repeated abuse that can result from such behaviors.

Setting proper boundaries with others is an area where children find change very difficult. They know how they were expected or allowed to act at home, and they may not have any idea what behaviors are unacceptable in your home. Therefore, children sometimes are unable to accept

and/or feel comfortable with what we consider normal relationships with family or friends. They need your clear guidance and support in the form of love, patience, teaching, and setting and enforcing expectations.

When children demonstrate inappropriate boundaries with others, it may present difficult situations for you as a Foster Parent. For example, foster children might try to cross over boundaries that properly separate you as a parent from the children in your home or try to violate the boundaries of your own children or other foster children in the home. Examples include children touching adults sexually, telling other children about explicit sexual behaviors, or trying to create tension between the foster parents by wanting an exclusive relationship with one of them.

Children who make poor choices about boundaries may be used to adults treating them as peers, friends, or as equals. These children have not been taught that in an appropriate adult-child relationship, adults must be authority figures, providing guidance and helping children meet their needs. As a Foster Parent, it is crucial for you to take on a clear "adult role" that defines you as a teacher, leader, and protector of the kids in your care. That doesn't mean you must become excessively strict or harsh with your foster child. You can be a responsible caregiver and an effective role model and still have a good relationship with the children in your care. Developing solid relationships with kids can open the lines of communication and help children be more open to you and your teaching.

## Benefits of Strong Relationships

When you develop strong relationships with your foster children, you help them learn and grow. Your foster children are more likely to spend time with you when relationships are healthy and strong. When a child seeks you out and wants to be with you, the entire teaching and learning process is made easier. In good relationships, children are more receptive to your teaching. Simply put, your foster child is more likely to listen to you, whether you are giving praise for positive behavior or correcting inappropriate behavior. As you and the child spend more time together, you will have many more opportunities to teach by example.

Furthermore, as relationships develop, children are more likely to understand and accept your values, rationales, and opinions. In this way, kids can receive the biggest benefit from you as a positive role model.

In addition to being exposed to positive role models and active help through teaching, foster children also need to be able to talk with you about how they are feeling and what they are thinking. When a relationship is sensitive and caring, a child is much more likely to share problems, concerns, joys, fears, and opinions. With frequent, open, and honest communication, it becomes easier for you to be sensitive to the needs of each child and to do what's best for him or her.

Developing a strong, healthy relationship also can have a positive impact on the choices kids make. You are never

certain how long a child will be in your foster home, but you can still have a positive influence by making that child feel cared for and loved. When this happens, a child might be less likely to become involved in using drugs, running away, or engaging in illegal activity.

As your foster children develop close ties with you, they begin to care about what you think of them. Over time, they will work harder to please you and the other important people in their lives (parents, teachers, clergy, and so on).

# Building Blocks of Relationships

Think about the qualities that make up any good relationship in your life. These qualities – respect, warmth, trust, and others – are the building blocks of positive relationships. If you use and model such qualities, you have the tools to build a solid relationship with your foster child. The following qualities can help you build positive, healthy relationships with kids in your home.

## Warmth

Many foster children have been hurt and disappointed by people who are important to them. As a result, they might not trust others or may have completely lost faith in both adults and peers.

As a Foster Parent, you can restore some of that trust by showing warmth. From the very first day a foster child comes into your home, make him or her feel welcome and part of the family. Ask questions and include the child in

conversations. Seek the child's opinion about family activities so he or she feels a sense of belonging. Get to know the child's likes and dislikes. You also can show warmth by taking time to talk with the child about simple things like how he or she likes his room or what video would be good to rent on Friday night. And let the child know he or she can come to you any time with questions or concerns. It's simply a matter of reaching out to the child in many small ways each day. These meaningful connections can make a huge difference in a child's life.

As mentioned earlier, some foster children may have boundary issues so showing warmth through touch may make them feel very uncomfortable. The best way to handle this is to ask the child if it is okay for you to give hugs or encouraging pats on the back. If they aren't comfortable with touching, you can always use a concerned voice tone and smiles to show that you care about a child and consider him or her part of your family.

## Listening

Much of our communication with other people is done without saying a word. Taking the time to listen to someone isn't always easy, but it is a way to demonstrate caring, interest, and warmth. Young people need to have someone who will listen to them. They might have a problem or they might just want to tell you about their day. Many kids have not yet learned how to appropriately express themselves. At times, they feel one way, while their words say something else. By listening carefully, you can pick up on cues that indicate what is troubling a young girl or boy.

Sometimes, you may have to restate or rephrase what the child said or ask questions to help him or her get to the root of the problem. You also can teach children to correctly identify and label feelings and emotions and explain how they affect behavior. At times, kids will say "off the wall" things just to get your attention or indicate that something is bothering them. A simple question like, *"Would you like to talk about it?"* can open the door to a meaningful interaction. You can really help a young person if you are attentive and listen, particularly if you learn to identify and take advantage of times when the children in your home are most open to and/or need to talk.

## Respect

Respect is an essential element in developing relationships. You must show children in your care that you respect who they are. You also must instill in them the importance of showing respect to others. This starts as soon as a child arrives at your home. Here are some ways you can show children that you respect them:

- Listen to them without judging or criticizing.
- Let them make their own decisions, when appropriate.
- Don't tease them about personal characteristics they are sensitive about. Examples include the way they look or talk, or personal problems like wetting the bed or learning disorders.
- Give them your full attention when they are talking to you.

- Respect their privacy and possessions. (Obviously, in dangerous situations, you would take the appropriate action as discussed in Chapter 4, "Creating a Safe Environment.")
- Respect their attachment to their family.
- Respect cultural differences.

Remember, respect is a two-way street. So, a foster child also must respect others. Some ways kids can do this include:

- Using good manners (saying *"Please"* and *"Thank you"*).
- Not arguing with you.
- Apologizing if they hurt someone.
- Asking to borrow someone else's possessions and returning borrowed items in good condition.
- Being nice to your own kids and pets.

It is important to note that the skill level of the kids who come into your home will vary. In other words, some foster kids may know many of these skills well, while others may need your help to learn how to do these things.

It is a huge confidence booster when young people know that you value and respect them. And children who feel good about their place in the world are less likely to use aggressive behaviors, victimize others, or use other inappropriate behaviors to get what they want.

## Concern and Understanding

Kids live in their "kid world," just as we live in our "adult world." Those worlds don't always exist in perfect harmony. Often, when kids try to explain a problem in their lives, adults say something like, *"That's not a problem. Wait until you're older, then you'll know what real problems are."* That's the same as saying, *"Go away kid, you're bothering me."*

As caregivers, we must try to see life from the child's perspective. For example, if a young person wants to share something with you, pay attention and listen. You should feel good that he or she trusts you enough to ask for your advice and help. Also, remember that all kids develop mentally, emotionally, and physically at different rates; treat each child as an individual. At every age and developmental stage of a child's life, new issues and problems arise. Show your concern by being supportive and listening carefully. What may seem like a minor problem to you can be a major problem to a young person.

## Appropriate Humor and Fun

There's a little kid in each of us, but some adults won't let that little kid out to play. Yet playing teaches valuable lessons about life, including sharing, respecting others, and how to relieve stress without getting "high" or hitting someone.

Having a good sense of humor can be an invaluable tool when working with children. Humor is an excellent way to build relationships with young people. It shows them that you are human and approachable. It's also a good way to model behavior. Kids need to learn how to find humor in life and to realize how healthy it is to laugh. They need a break from their stress just as much as adults do.

For adults, caring for kids can be a tough business, one that's full of ups and downs. If you find humor in what happens each day, you are less likely to dwell on the bad things that might happen with you and your foster child. Finding humor in everyday events helps make your home and relationship with your foster child more pleasant. A good sense of humor can help you deal with and overcome the negative events and feelings that can often get the best of you.

You don't have to be a stand-up comedian to use humor with foster children. The point is to let them know that you have a sense of humor; this can help make you more approachable. Use the type of humor that suits your personality. Maybe you're a good story-teller and can use funny stories to teach the lessons you want to teach. Or perhaps your sense of humor leans more toward the use of exaggeration and understatement. If so, you can bring a smile to a young person's face with remarks like *"He must have eaten a bazillion tacos"* or *"I'm so broke, I can't even pay attention."*

> As caregivers, we must try to see life from the child's perspective.

While humor is a valuable relationship-building tool, it is important not to use humor that offends others or that reinforces problems that your foster child is having. For example, if you have a habit of making "smart" or "cute" comments when someone asks you to do something, it might be best not to do this with a child who already has a tendency to "wise off" to teachers or doesn't know when, where, and with whom such remarks are appropriate. Likewise, caustic humor, name-calling, or trash talking – even if done between adults – is not an appropriate type of humor to use in front of your foster child. Remember, as you become a favorite role model for your foster kids, have fun with them but don't model or teach humor that could be used in inappropriate ways and/or at inappropriate times.

Whatever type of humor you use, it's important to make it a natural extension of your personality. In this way, humor provides welcome relief from the everyday stresses of life and allows us to relax and enjoy each other. Don't be afraid to let children express their sense of humor. Appropriate jokes and gentle teasing are a natural part of life and they can have a place in your home.

## Empathy and Trustworthiness

Empathy means being sensitive to others by trying to understand their situation and feelings. For many people, this is not easy or natural. Many of us grew up being told what we should do and how we should feel. In fact, some of us have trouble identifying our own true feelings. Maybe you've heard statements like *"You really don't mean that"* or *"There's no reason to feel that way; straighten up and fly right."*

Although these statements may be appropriate on rare occasions, they don't have much effect on changing a young person's behavior for the better. Oftentimes, the harder you try to convince children that they really aren't feeling what they say they're feeling, the more those feelings seem to stick.

Kids go through many changes as they grow, and they often don't know how to handle new experiences and the emotions that these changes bring. Sometimes, they may feel trapped by their feelings and think that any attempt to change is worthless. As hard as you try, it often will be difficult for you to understand some of the experiences and frustrations that foster children have been through or are currently encountering. For many of them, change – no matter how good it looks initially – can lead to fear that things will not turn out the way they want.

You can steer the young people in your care through the minefield of emotions by validating their feelings and by assuring them that the confusion, sadness, or anger that they are experiencing is perfectly okay and normal for their situation. At the same time, however, you must teach them that how they act on those feelings can have an impact – positive or negative – on themselves or others.

Kids need to learn that negative emotions are a temporary part of life and that things will get better. You can teach them that it's okay to feel bad sometimes; more importantly, you can help them find the strength in themselves to carry on. In this way, you can help youngsters begin the process of hope and healing.

We all know that it's easy to talk to a young person when he or she is happy and has a positive outlook. Dealing constructively with a child's negative feelings requires much more skill and patience. This can be a great time to use empathy. It requires you to look at the world through the eyes of your foster child. In order to use empathy better, think about how you felt in similar situations. It will probably never be the same, but you can get a good idea of what your foster child is going through and figure out how best to approach and help him or her.

Many young people, especially those who are aggressive and violent, also face the problem of not having a trusted adult in their lives. This may be because an adult betrayed a child's trust, or because the child's negative behaviors have pushed away the adult in his or her life. In addition, more foster children than ever before are coming from dysfunctional or abusive backgrounds where they haven't received the love and discipline they need. These kids need someone they can talk to about

**Kids need to learn that negative emotions are a temporary part of life and that things will get better.**

their fear and pain. They may not know how to do it appropriately. You may have to look for signs – subtle and otherwise – that they're ready to share their feelings and encourage them to do so.

Once you have established a solid relationship with your foster child, you'll be able to talk frankly with him or her about the importance of asking for help. Many times, young people are embarrassed to seek help, especially if the problem is a personal one. Or they may prejudge that you are like all the other adults they have known. They may think you are not capable of understanding them or will put them down. By developing a trusting relationship, you can let them know that you and others who care about them are always available. Then, you can teach them that it's better to seek advice from a trusted person than to take an action that might hurt someone or make the situation worse.

Remember that empathy does not replace teaching and consequences. Kids need to learn that feeling bad is not an excuse for misbehavior. Just because a child is angry with the teacher, doesn't mean the child can call him or her names or hit someone. As a Foster Parent, you may have empathy for a child who is going through a difficult time, but that doesn't mean you should protect the child from the consequences that come from his or her inappropriate behavior. Some adults rush to solve a child's problem. They feel that supplying all of the answers is their primary role. While giving advice and instructions is very important, there are times when it's best to just listen or for the child to experience the natural consequences of his or her behavior.

Psychologist Steven Covey challenges us to seek first to understand and then to be understood. This is particularly important when working with children in foster care. Foster Parents must realize that these kids have had many experiences that are not healthy and that they are very likely to interpret life experiences quite differently than we do.

Constantly rushing to offer a solution can be a real turn-off to young people. There are times in life when each of us merely wants to feel that someone is on our side. As you build relationships with your foster child, you will learn to gauge when and where to offer solutions or empathy. In other chapters in this book, we will discuss methods for helping young people learn to take responsibility for their own problems and how to develop skills to solve these problems.

## Praise and Encouragement

Praise is nourishment. It helps young people grow emotionally, just as food helps them grow physically. Remember to be specific with your praise at first, then move on to more generalized praise. Praise behavior so that your foster child fully understands how to continue the good behavior. For example, when you first start working with a foster child, say things like *"Jamie, thanks for getting ready so quickly this morning. Now we will be able to get to school on time."* In this way, Jamie knows exactly what behaviors you approve of and want to see again.

As children begin to adopt positive behaviors, you can gradually begin to praise more generally and sporadically. Sometimes, a simple statement like, *"Good job!"* is enough to help your foster child understand that you continue to approve of his or her behavior. Kids make progress at different rates, and your praise should be adjusted to fit their age and developmental level. Also, you can show your appreciation to a child by pointing out his or her positive qualities with comments like, *"Boy, you really stick with a job until it's done!"* Respect the uniqueness of your kids and recognize what makes each of them feel worthwhile and accepted.

> Praise is nourishment. It helps young people grow emotionally.

Remember to be brief and enthusiastic when you praise a child, and offer praise at appropriate times. Usually, it's best to praise kids immediately, but there may be situations where it's better to wait. For example, some young people don't like to be praised in front of others because it embarrasses them. You might give these kids a "thumbs up" or a simple head nod to show approval. Other kids, however, are encouraged more with words. Take the time to get to know your kids, and you'll find the right formula for praise. (We'll discuss specific ways to praise children later in this book.)

## Summary

As you work with your foster child, remember that one of the central concepts of the Girls and Boys Town Teaching Model, and any effective foster parenting approach, is the presence of positive, appropriate relationships between children and adults. These relationships can take hard work on everyone's part, especially in foster care, where children may bring with them a complex history of experiences. As a Foster Parent, keep in mind that the real goal of building positive relationships is not to be liked as a peer by the child, but rather to be liked and respected as a caring, consistent adult.

# CHAPTER 2

# The Professional Foster Parent

When most people think of Foster Parents, they think of a family that provides a home to children who can't live with their own families for a while. These Foster Parents are expected to care for the child's basic needs and treat him or her kindly. Period.

However, as a Foster Parent, you know that caring for foster children involves much more than just providing them with food and a place to sleep. Some of today's foster children come to you with tough problems. And an important part of being a professional Foster Parent is realizing that kids require more than just basic care; they also need understanding, nurturing, and guidance. Being a professional Foster Parent requires commitment and patience.

What does it mean to be a professional Foster Parent? How does this change your parenting role, and what responsibilities do you accept?

Professionals are generally viewed as experts who are competent, caring, and cooperative. By using the professional behaviors discussed in this chapter, Foster Parents earn respect for themselves, their home, and the program they represent. More importantly, foster children will receive better care.

Part of becoming a professional Foster Parent means that you agree to live by a code of acceptable behaviors and ethics. Some of these include:

1. Making Sure the Child Receives Humane Treatment
2. Being a Good Role Model
3. Respecting Cultural Diversity
4. Working as a Team
5. Continuing to Develop Professional Skills
6. Giving and Receiving Suggestions and Advice
7. Communicating Clearly and Effectively
8. Maintaining Confidentiality
9. Advocating for the Foster Child

## Making Sure the Child Receives Humane Treatment

Caring for foster children can be stressful and hectic. By thoughtfully providing humane treatment, you can develop a warm, loving relationship with them and keep the stress level in your home to a minimum.

Foster Parents are strongly encouraged to work with and help the kids in their care *every day*. This means focusing on teaching children life skills they may need help

with, and using logical, positive and negative consequences you and your agency have agreed on ahead of
time.

Being a professional also means that you agree to work
within the rules of your program and not "do your own
thing." This means using the skills you are taught in your
initial training and following the policies and procedures
of your program.

## Being a Good Role Model

As professionals, Foster Parents are role models for
their foster children and for other Foster Parents. When
you "practice what you preach," you show your commitment to the foster child and your confidence in what you
are teaching. Furthermore, you can demonstrate and help
your foster child learn a variety of skills, like using appropriate humor, expressing anger
without hurting anyone, being
sensitive to the needs of others,
asking for help when appropriate, and many others. These all
are skills you can teach and
model to your foster child.

> Being a
> professional
> Foster Parent
> requires
> commitment
> and patience.

Appropriate modeling also
comes into play when you meet
with professionals from other agencies, schools, courts,
and so on. It's important to show respect to your foster
child by avoiding negative labeling or using words like
"brat," "mean," "stupid," or "lazy" when talking about the

child with these other professionals. (See the chart "Labels and Behaviors.") While you never plan to use words like this, when you're under a lot of stress, they can slip out. Using slang or jargon can affect the child's self-confidence and how others view him or her.

Instead, it is more professional and helpful to your foster child if you specifically describe the behaviors he or she needs to learn. Although this takes a little longer to say or even to think of, it is more specific, focuses on what the child needs to learn, and describes what you or others can do to help the child.

---

## Labels and Behaviors

*For each negative label, there is a professional way to specifically describe a child's behaviors.*

| Label | Behavior(s) |
|---|---|
| Instead of "brat" | Use: argues, doesn't follow instructions, talks back, etc. |
| Instead of "mean" | Use: physically aggressive, makes negative comments, etc. |
| Instead of "stupid" | Use: has difficulty with schoolwork, sometimes needs help understanding instructions, etc. |
| Instead of "lazy" | Use: doesn't complete chores, refuses to take part in family activities, etc. |

---

Other professional behaviors to model include dressing appropriately, using correct grammar and good listening skills, being on time for meetings, and completing tasks when you say you will. (When delays are unavoidable and commitments cannot be kept, Foster Parents should always let others know, request a new timeline, and be sure to meet it.)

Doing the things discussed in this section will help set you apart as a professional Foster Parent and provide your foster child with a much-needed positive role model.

## Respecting Cultural Diversity

Being a Foster Parent provides you with an exciting opportunity to teach children a wide variety of social, academic, and life skills. It is equally important, however, for you to understand and appreciate each child's family, religious, ethnic, and cultural background. This means valuing differences, becoming educated about them, and presenting them to your own family as a positive learning experience.

Ethnic and cultural sensitivity is essential for those who care for children from different cultures. In today's diverse society, it is likely that Foster Parents will take foster children into their homes from other cultures and backgrounds. So, cultural awareness and sensitivity are important in helping children get better while in your care. These factors require that you become more knowledgeable about ethnic and cultural differences and address biases you may have.

Research has defined various ways for caregivers to achieve the goal of becoming culturally skilled. Derald Wing Sue and David Sue (1990), two respected researchers on this subject, state that culturally skilled caregivers are working toward three goals:

1. They are actively becoming aware of their own assumptions about human behavior, values, biases, and stereotypes.

2. They attempt to understand the world views and values of children from other cultures.

3. The culturally skilled caregiver develops and practices appropriate and sensitive intervention strategies in his or her work with children from other cultures.

Let's look at how these goals can be accomplished.

The first goal involves becoming aware of and understanding one's own assumptions about human behavior, values, biases, beliefs, and attitudes in one's own culture. This means realizing that the way you live and act, how you were brought up, your values, and so on, is only one way of living and that people live in other ways – not necessarily better or worse, just different. When you understand your own family's customs and traditions, you are better able to appreciate the customs and traditions of children from other cultures in your care. According to the researchers, culturally skilled caregivers have developed five characteristics in these areas:

1. **They have moved from being culturally unaware to being aware of and sensitive to their own cultural heritage.** At the same time, there is an acceptance and respect for cultural differences. These caregivers consider other cultures equally as valuable and legitimate as their own. The danger of being culturally unaware is cultural oppression – that is, imposing one's own cultural values and standards onto a child from another culture.

2. **Caregivers are aware of their own values and biases and how they may affect children from other cultures.** They try to avoid prejudices, unwarranted labeling, preconceived limitations or notions, and stereotyping.

3. **Culturally skilled caregivers are comfortable with the differences that exist between themselves and the children they care for in terms of race and beliefs.** They also accept that there are differences in attitudes, behaviors, and beliefs between cultures. They are not "colorblind." The idea of "colorblindness" refers to the belief that regardless of color or other physical differences, we all are people of humanity, and each individual is equally human. The danger here is that a caregiver may deny that there are differences between racial or cultural groups. He or she may send the message, *"I like you because I believe we are the same,"* rather than, *"I like you even though we are different."*

4. **Culturally skilled caregivers are aware of their limitations in dealing with a child from a different culture.** They don't hesitate to ask for help from someone who is more knowledgeable about or skilled in working with a particular culture. For example, a Foster Parent may ask for help in understanding how to care for a child's skin or hair, family relationship roles, or language differences.

5. **Culturally skilled caregivers are aware of and acknowledge the existence of their own prejudices, attitudes, and feelings.** They understand that everyone has prejudices, beliefs, and feelings to some degree, and they deal with them in a nondefensive, guilt-free manner.

The second goal listed by the researchers involves understanding the child's world view and values. This doesn't mean that you must adopt the views and values themselves, but rather accept them in a nonjudgmental manner. To be culturally skilled, a person must possess specific knowledge and information about a child. This involves trying to learn the history, experiences, cultural values, roles, and lifestyles of various cultural groups. The greater the depth of understanding, the more likely the caregiver is to be effective in helping the child. Thus, the culturally skilled person continues to explore and learn about issues related to different cultural groups throughout his or her professional career.

The third goal in becoming a culturally skilled caregiver is to treat each child individually. There is no "generic" way to care for all children. Treating each child individually is necessary not only because there are individual learning styles and histories, but also because of individual cultural factors. Cultural factors should be dealt with in an upfront fashion, and not ignored, when caring for a child. All peoples – Caucasian, African-American, Asian, Hispanic, and others – are different, and this must be taken into consideration. Acknowledging differences is not racist.

> Cultural awareness and sensitivity are important in helping children get better while in your care.

Knowledge of cultures that are different from your own is essential for effective care. You need to become aware of the experiences, values, and lifestyles inherent in other cultures. Only in this way can you expect to have a positive impact on a child in your care. Remember: Culturally skilled Foster Parents will treat a foster child as an individual first, regardless of the child's cultural background.

## Working as a Team

Foster Parents need to work with a variety of people when they become Foster Parents. In general, this includes caseworkers, court personnel, teachers or school administrators, the child's parents, therapists, and, especially, the foster child.

41

For a child to receive proper care, all these people must work together. One of your responsibilities is to work cooperatively with all of them. There are a number of general guidelines that can help you begin and maintain relationships with these people. These guidelines, along with the importance of good written and verbal communication, are reviewed in this section.

## Beginning Relationships

Help others understand your role by describing the agency that placed the child with you to people who may not know much about it. This includes explaining the program's approach to and philosophy of foster care. Express concern for the child and appreciation for the person's involvement.

Emphasize how much you value and need suggestions – positive and corrective – to help the child get the best care possible. Encourage communication by phone, letters, electronic mail, or visits.

## Maintaining Relationships

Talk with consumers regularly, share good news, and ask their opinions about how they think the child is doing. When you are given information about the child or your performance as a Foster Parent, thank the consumer for his or her concern and opinion. A pleasant, professional response helps ensure that the person will continue to communicate with you.

Show courtesy by calling ahead for appointments, being on time, and dressing appropriately. Present your information clearly and get to the point promptly. Ask for information in a nonthreatening manner, listen without interrupting, and ask for suggestions.

## School Contacts

Foster Parents should be very involved in a child's school program. In order for you to understand a child's educational needs, frequent contact with teachers through phone calls, meetings, school notes, and/or classroom observations can help you gather information. Regular communication with teachers also helps you determine how well the child is using skills taught at home in school. Finally, staying informed about the child's progress in school helps you to better develop and review the child's educational progress.

## Mental Health Providers

Some children in foster care may receive services from mental health providers (psychiatrists, psychologists, therapists, etc.). When working with these professionals, remember to respect their skills, training, and ability to provide special therapeutic assistance to the foster child. Mental health providers can help children resolve issues like loss, trauma, depression, and other issues that are beyond your expertise. Working together with mental health providers can help your foster child, so make an effort to be open and honest with them and to provide them with accurate information.

When a foster child is receiving services from a mental health specialist, it is important for Foster Parents and other people (parents) to understand the type of treatment the child is receiving. You should feel free to ask the mental health specialist questions so that you can be knowledgeable about the treatment the child is receiving and how it can be coordinated with the care you are providing in your home. If you feel that a mental health specialist is not able to satisfactorily answer your questions, is unwilling to listen to your information and input, or is offering treatment that doesn't seem to be helping the child, talk with your program supervisor. You are a part of a team, and everyone's ideas need to be heard.

## Continuing to Develop Professional Skills

As society changes, the needs of children change. Foster care has come to represent a broad array of services because the needs of children vary widely. In order to meet this increasing challenge, it's important that you continue to develop your professional skills. Some ways to do this include attending regular training or seminars, reading about new developments in foster care, learning more about how children develop and the issues they might encounter, and joining and participating in professional foster care organizations.

## Giving and Receiving Suggestions and Advice

For professional growth to occur, Foster Parents must *value, request,* and *respond* to suggestions and advice from others. This allows you to grow professionally and, ultimately, succeed as a Foster Parent.

Suggestions and advice can be used to let someone know what they are doing well or to help correct a problem or an inappropriate behavior. If suggestions and advice are shared on a day-to-day basis, everyone – Foster Parents and foster children – learns and grows.

Naturally, most people would prefer to only give and receive positive suggestions and advice. In reality we all have behaviors that may hinder us from doing our best. And, other people might feel uncomfortable talking about these behaviors. Examples of such behaviors are being late to appointments, using inappropriate language around children, or gossiping about a child's family problems. Many people are not used to receiving corrective information about their behaviors. They may feel offended or insulted because they think they are being criticized personally. That's why it is important for Foster Parents to understand that the goal of giving and receiving suggestions and advice is to improve themselves professionally so that foster kids receive the best care possible.

**Remember: Corrective suggestions and advice can help you improve your skills and job performance, so don't view them as personal attacks.** You were selected to be a Foster Parent because you have solid judgment, the ability to nurture and provide a safe environment, and a commitment to helping children. No matter how good you are at these things, no one expects you to be perfect. You can always improve on how you provide quality care to foster children. One of the best ways to do this is through learning to accept others' evaluations of your skills – both positive and corrective – as vehicles to help you become a better Foster Parent.

## Communicating Clearly and Effectively

Clear, frequent, and pleasant communication is an important hallmark of professionalism. With it, work can be completed smoothly. Without it, confusion and misunderstandings develop and often result in unpleasant and unproductive working relationships.

One communication skill that certainly will help you is being positive. A positive, "can do" attitude is respected and appreciated. Someone who cheerfully takes on new tasks, doesn't complain, and recognizes and praises the work and achievements of others is a valued member of any professional group.

As Foster Parents, it's important to have a close working relationship with the people in your program. To do this, you should frequently communicate with them and with other people helping the child, especially early in a child's placement. This might include face-to-face meetings and/or phone calls to discuss the child's behaviors and needs.

Foster Parents also should communicate openly and honestly with program personnel about personal or professional issues that may affect their ability to care for a foster child. Program staff should understand that Foster Parents are real people, and that real people have problems and frustrations from time to time. Staff members can provide more effective help if you trust them with your frustrations or concerns.

It's important to keep in mind that when people work together, relationships remain respectful and, ultimately, children get the care they deserve.

## Maintaining Confidentiality

Foster Parents have access to a great deal of information about each child and his or her family, and background. Because of the sensitive nature of some of this information, they must be careful about sharing it with others. Confidential information should be shared only with persons who have a legitimate need for it and a right to it. This varies from state to state, so it's important for you to learn your state's protocols concerning this issue. If you want to maintain professional relationships with everyone involved with the foster child, confidentiality is a must. Doing this preserves your integrity and develops a sense of trust among the child in your care, the program, and consumers. As a rule, the positive accomplishments of a child should be shared with others, but individual child problems should be discussed only with the appropriate individuals. Speak with your program supervisor to decide what information about your

> Confidential information should be shared only with persons who have a legitimate need for it and a right to it.

foster child can be shared with others (school personnel, therapist).

The following examples show the right way and the wrong way to respond to someone's questions about confidential information.

## Examples

Your brother-in-law asks you, *"Why do you think Michael's parents put him in the hospital? I heard he tried to hurt himself."*

> **Unprofessional response:** *"Yeah, Michael has had a lot of trouble. He's been depressed and has thought about hurting himself. His psychiatrist said he was getting better."*

> **Professional response:** *"I appreciate your interest in Michael, but the reasons he is in our home are private. Would you mind if Michael practiced his basketball shots on your hoop until we get one up this weekend?"*

The school nurse says, *"I heard Sara was at the police station talking to the police about some sexual problems in the family. What did they tell you about this?"*

> **Unprofessional response:** *"They told me that her dad might have been sexually abusing her and her older sister, too. The sister had a baby a few years ago, but I think she gave it to another family to raise. I think the whole family has trouble."*

**Professional response:** *"I appreciate you_
*for Sara, but I can't discuss any of th*
*she's in our care."*

Your neighbor says, *"I really am amazed that you would
be willing to let that boy (your foster son) in your home.
I've heard that he has been causing trouble for years. I
heard that he was yelling at some teachers at the school
last week. Is that true?"*

> **Unprofessional response:** *"Michael thought the
> teacher was 'on him' too much. He can really get
> mad sometimes. I think his dad used to yell a lot
> and that is where Michael learned it. His dad
> has a pretty bad drinking problem from what I
> understand."*

> **Professional response:** *"We enjoy having Michael
> in our home. He's really a neat kid."* (The Foster
> Parent politely excuses himself or herself.)

Your best friend watched your kids for you while you went
through some training classes. When your new foster child,
John, moves in, she says, *"I really admire your willingness
to be a Foster Parent. But has he been involved in gangs?
He sure has a lot of tattoos. Don't you worry that he'll be
a bad influence on your own kids?"*

> **Unprofessional response:** *"Yeah, he's been in a
> gang for about a year now. I think we got him
> just when he was going to be initiated. He want-*

*ed to get out but he didn't know how. His aunt helped raise him. She works at City Hall."*

**Professional response:** *"You were really a big help to us when we were in training. Thanks for watching our kids. But John's history is private and something we can't talk about."*

## Advocating for the Foster Child

To "get along" with people, Foster Parents shouldn't merely "go along" with what other people want. You must be willing to advocate for the best interests of your foster child, just as you would for your own children.

The concept of "assertive advocacy" should guide all your activities when you interact with teachers, program personnel, police, and others who share responsibility for the child. Advocate for a foster child in ways that don't alienate people or close off channels of communication. That is what professionalism is all about.

## Summary

Foster Parents play an important role in helping children have a chance to enjoy happy and satisfying lives. This chapter has presented some essential professional skills that will help ensure that foster children have positive experiences in your care. Making sure the child receives humane treatment, modeling positive and professional behavior, respecting cultural diversity, working as a team, continuing to develop professional skills, giving and receiving suggestions and advice, communicating effectively, maintaining confidentiality, and advocating for your foster child are key elements in providing effective care. Using these professional skills and embracing the values explained in this chapter will help both you and your foster child reach your goals.

# CHAPTER 3

# Working with a Foster Child's Family

As a professional, you must remember that just as there is no such thing as a "perfect parent," no parent *wants* to be a poor parent. But many parents lack the knowledge or motivation to develop the skills necessary to be a successful parent after their children are placed in foster care. An important part of a Foster Parent's job involves helping parents learn these skills and supporting the other professionals who are helping the foster child's parents.

While it is important for a child's family to be part of his or her life, Foster Parents should be aware that they may face situations where it is necessary to work with parents or family members who have neglected or physically or sexually abused a child. If a foster child brings these issues with him or her, your natural reaction might be strong feelings of shock, anger, or revulsion toward these family members. You must put these feelings aside and keep your focus on what is best for the child. You may not like what the family has done, but it is still important to respect the foster child's attachment to the original family. Remember that you cannot effectively do your job and truly help children if you only listen and react to your own emotions.

## Parents Should Be Part of the Team

One of your main goals as a Foster Parent is to help foster children have the best possible relationship with their families. Helping your foster child maintain a good relationship with his or her family is important – regardless of whether the child will be returning home or adopted – for two very important reasons.

### Attachment Significance

Our families are our families for life. As was discussed earlier, foster children often develop their primary attachment to one or both of their parents, and this profoundly affects the way they view themselves. If a child is attached to parents who feel good about themselves, the child learns self-respect. If a child is attached to parents who don't feel good about themselves, the child may feel low self-worth. When you help a child's parents become more confident and positive about their ability to care for themselves and their children, the children benefit by having opportunities to become emotionally attached to positive role models instead of negative ones who make them question their own value.

### Reunification

Many foster children return to their own family or to the home of another relative. Therefore, in order to best help the child, you have a duty to help make the environment to which the child will be returning as supportive and helpful as possible. You can do this, in part, by teaching the parents or guardians parenting skills they don't have. For example, you can model how you use praise to increase the child's positive behaviors. Additionally, by including the parents in the child's permanency planning, everyone benefits from the parents' knowledge of the child. Finally, when the parents learn about the services and service providers that are currently helping the child, they will have more knowledge about what the child will need when he or she eventually returns home.

## Building Relationships with a Child's Family

As Foster Parents, you can make several important contributions to helping your foster child's family. Most of these contributions focus on building a trusting, comfortable relationship. This allows you and the child's family to exchange valuable information and also gives you the opportunity to teach or model positive parenting skills and behaviors. All of these factors are essential in moving a child and his or her family toward reunification. Following are some ways you can help your foster child's parents.

### Building a Relationship

Provide support and understanding to the family and build relationships. Foster Parents can be very positive role models for their foster child's parents. Can you think of people in your life who are positive role models for you?

Before you decided that these were people you wanted to be like, you probably developed a relationship with them that allowed you to learn more about their values, abilities, and personalities. As a result of this relationship, you learned to value the way they lived their lives. You may have consulted them when you had a problem or decision to make because you knew they made sound decisions.

**It is important to respect the foster child's attachment to the original family.**

This is also true for the families of foster children. Before they decide to accept some of your suggestions for parenting their child during visits or when he or she returns home, they need to get to know you. After they develop a relationship with you, to the extent that is possible, they will be more likely to trust your judgment and suggestions about how to parent.

You can encourage parents to develop this relationship with you by listening to their suggestions and explanations about the child's unique needs and personality. By doing this, you help affirm the parents' ability to understand and their desire to help their own child. Although you may not agree with all of the parents' values or personal decisions, it is very important to look for positive attempts on their part to help and stay involved with their child. Many parents can be isolated and have a small support system. They may seem cautious when you initially meet them because they feel that they have been labeled "bad parents" and you are the "good parents." But if you persist in being pleasant and offering them common courtesies, they will probably decide to trust you more and eventually may want to listen to your suggestions.

## Showing Empathy

Be empathetic with the parents' feelings of temporary loss of the child from the family. Listen, make eye contact, smile. What you do is as important as what you say. Some parents will remain angry that their child was placed in foster care against their wishes. You don't have to defend or explain why the foster child was placed. Listening in general is an important tool in developing a relationship with anyone and will help you get to know the child's parents. Expressing understanding of their sense of loss may help them feel that you are there not to judge them but to support them.

## Providing Parenting Opportunities

Give parents opportunities to parent their own kids. This can be hard to do. If you know the parents have abused or neglected their child in the past, it is hard not to worry about how they will treat the child now. But even if the visits are completely supervised, the parent should still have the opportunity to do some parenting. This could include simple activities like brushing the child's hair, giving a snack, or stopping an argument. This gives parents an opportunity to "practice" new skills they are learning or to use skills they already have.

Most of the time, parents will feel like they're "playing second fiddle" to you. Most of their power or respect as a parent has been taken away, and they often will feel intimidated or inadequate, or feel like they are competing against you. They may not attempt to do much parenting when you are around because they don't want to have their decisions or actions compared to yours. However, if you express confidence in them and praise them for the good things they do for their child, parents can develop more confidence and will be more likely to continue to take on the parenting role when they are with the child.

This is good for the parent as well as for the child. No matter how well you take care of your foster children, you are not their "real" parent. Although you care for and may love your foster children, you cannot replace their desire to be loved by their own parents. Kids express this longing differently at different ages, but it is never completely gone. You hope that someday a child's parents can love him or her the way the child wants them to, and part of your job is to encourage and strengthen the love between them. It is important to remember that foster children have membership in another family by birth and will at times prefer that family to yours.

## Being Approachable

Because you provide care for your foster child, the parents may begin to see you as the "expert" who really knows how to parent or set limits with their child. You will start to figure out what works and what doesn't work with this particular foster child. This will become especially clear when you begin to have some success in helping the foster child change his or her behaviors. Parents may ask you for advice about how to respond to certain behaviors their child displays during visits. You can tell the parents how you would handle it and ask if they think it would work for them. You also can reinforce the parents' belief that they too have some valuable parenting skills by identifying some of the child's strengths the parents have already taught. For instance, you could say, *"John always gets up when his alarm clock rings. How did you teach him to do that?"* Or you could find out more about the family's way of responding to a certain behavior and let the parents know that it worked in the foster home, too.

## Modeling Parenting Skills

Model and teach effective parenting skills. Modeling is a very powerful teaching tool. When the foster child's parents see you handle misbehavior without hitting, screaming, or withdrawing, they may begin to think you know something that they may want to learn. Not all parents will get on the bandwagon, but some will. Those parents who are ready and willing to learn better parenting skills will watch you carefully and, with support, will want to try to do what they see works in your family. As we mentioned earlier, parents will be more likely to accept your suggestions if they feel they have a sincere and honest relationship with you.

While modeling and teaching are important, you must exercise some caution. As discussed earlier, parents must have opportunities to parent their own children. Use your judgment to determine whether a child's parents are receptive to what you are teaching, and whether you are taking away their opportunity to interact with their children.

> Although you care for and may love your foster children, you cannot replace their desire to be loved by their own parents.

Anyone who is a parent can appreciate that we all need some help from time to time. Most of us know that using resources in the community makes our job a lot easier and makes us more successful. Modeling for the foster child's parents how to use community resources can open up another source of assistance for the child's parents. You can show parents how to call the doctor for an appointment, how to give medicine appropriately, how to advocate for their child to get the help he or she needs at school, or how to choose a day care agency. The list is endless. As you get to know your foster child better, you will learn which resources help you, and you can transfer that knowledge to your foster child's parents.

## Developing the Child's Skills

By teaching positive skill development, you will help the child have a better chance of being successful when he or she returns home. For instance, when your foster daughter improves her ability to accept "No" answers or to use the *P-O-P* problem-solving method (explained in Chapter 17), she is more likely to respond to her parents' instructions and make better decisions.

Working with foster children ahead of time on new social skills that they can use during home visits will help them have the best visit possible. By supporting the children and helping them have positive visits with their parents, they will feel your acceptance of their families as a whole. This in turn will help the children feel better about themselves.

## Not Taking Criticism Personally

It is hard not to take personally a parent's jealousy of you or your role as a foster child's primary caretaker. It's important to understand, though, that many parents would feel defensive if someone else – a stranger – was chosen to parent their child. Try to remember that parents are very aware that you are doing the job that they should be doing. They may try to undercut you with comments suggesting, for example, that you should have sent a coat with the foster child during a visit, or that you should have taken a child with a cold to the doctor. Don't let this get under your skin. Some parents would feel jealous of whomever was chosen to care for their children, whether it was you or someone else. Most of us would feel much the same way if we were in those parents' shoes.

If a parent's criticism is an ongoing problem, you may mention to him or her that you are doing the best job you can. Do this only when your foster child is not around. The message you are sending may not help the parent change but may begin to help him or her see that you are doing your best to help the child.

## Encouraging Family Involvement

Keep the family and the child "connected" when family visits or a return home is a goal. Foster Parents can encourage parents to keep their child involved with the family by arranging visits (when possible), and helping the family continue to celebrate holidays, birthdays, and other important events together. Having the parents meet all those involved in their child's care before the child is actually placed is extremely important. This tells the parents that their information and relationship are valuable and needed by you, and that no one is "counting them out."

Other ways to support families include the following: teaching children social skills that will help them have pleasant visits with their parents; suggesting that the parents visit when the child is rested or doesn't have to get up early for school the next morning after an evening visit; praising the parents for being on time for visits or reporting information to you about how a visit went; and thanking parents for making suggestions about the child's care (food allergies, hobbies, ways to comfort the child when he or she is upset).

> **Teach children social skills that will help them have pleasant visits with their parents.**

If the foster child is getting ready to move home, it is especially important for parents to attend school conferences, doctor appointments, and other meetings so that the transition is as smooth as possible for the child. A successful reunification is most likely if the child's family and the child feel that the foster family is willing to help them work toward this goal and supports it.

## Summary

While Foster Parents might think it would be easier to have little or no contact with their foster child's family, there are actually many short-term and long-term benefits of working together. Not only do both families benefit from exchanging information, but the child also experiences more continuity in his or her life. If your foster child returns to live with his or her parents, the parents may be willing to use many of the parenting techniques the Foster Parents have found helpful. Everyone wins!

# CHAPTER 4

# Creating a Safe Environment

One of the fundamental responsibilities of being a parent is creating a safe environment for children. When they are toddlers, we put plastic protectors in electrical sockets so they will not get shocked. We watch carefully as they take their first steps so they won't fall. We buy bicycle helmets when they graduate from tricycles to bikes with training wheels. We teach them about using seat belts as soon as they're big enough to wear one, and help them practice safe driving habits when they are teenagers.

Unfortunately, we cannot assume that children who enter foster care have lived in a protective environment or have been taught the things they need to know to remain safe. As a Foster Parent, you may encounter these everyday safety concerns, as well as a wide range of other challenges. Children in foster care may have been victims of physical, sexual, and psychological abuse. Drugs and alcohol may play a large and destructive role in their lives and in the lives of their families. Many environmental factors, such as poverty, also could be at work.

So how can you ensure that you are creating a safe environment for the children in your foster home? One way is to clearly state to foster children their rights and ensure that they, and you, understand these rights. Girls and Boys Town has developed a list of child rights that help ensure the care a child receives is safe and promotes growth. Some of these rights resulted from laws or court decisions. (Most of these court decisions dealt with and involved older children. The practices used with younger children may vary due to their age and developmental needs.)

> **Children have the right to live in an environment that is safe and promotes spiritual, emotional, intellectual, and physical growth.**

Some grew out of our more than 80 years of experience caring for thousands of children at Girls and Boys Town. All of these rights are built around caring for children in the least-restrictive way possible.

The rights covered here are examples that provide Foster Parents with concepts about how to ensure a safe environment and not violate a foster child's rights. It would be impossible to list every instance where a rights violation may be an issue. The concepts are presented as a way to give Foster Parents an understanding and general framework in order to make good judgments when working with foster children.

Girls and Boys Town believes that children have the right to live in an environment that is safe and promotes spiritual, emotional, intellectual, and physical growth. Our approach to promoting safe environments is built into all of our programs. The following list includes the four components we use to create and promote a safe environment for the children in our care. These components are an integral part of our Treatment Family Foster Care Program and can easily be incorporated into any foster care program and used by its Foster Parents:

Policies and Procedures

Training in Positive Interaction Styles

Regular Foster Child Interviews

Training in the Rights of Foster Children

## Policies and Procedures

The commitment to provide safe environments for foster children begins here. Each Foster Parent is made aware of written policies and procedures related to protecting the rights of children. These policies and procedures emphasize the intent of the program and spell out the procedures that are to be followed when possible policy violations occur. Policies and procedures set in motion other specific actions that are required of staff members and Foster Parents. It's important to remember that violating rights can damage relationships. On the other hand, ensuring children's rights can provide a foundation where healthy relationships can flourish.

## Training in Positive Interaction Styles

All Foster Parents are trained in positive ways to interact with and help foster children change their behaviors, while respecting their basic dignity and freedom. Foster Parents also are trained in promoting positive relationships with foster children by using *Effective Praise* (see Chapter 13) and other relationship-building strategies.

## Regular Foster Child Interviews

Each foster child is interviewed throughout placement as well as when he or she leaves the program. During these interviews, children are asked about their care, how supportive the Foster Parents were, and the overall effectiveness of the care they received. Information from these interviews can provide important information about the home's atmosphere, including whether or not it is a good, safe place for children to live. This information will benefit other children placed in the home.

## Training in the Rights of Foster Children

All Girls and Boys Town Foster Parents receive training to increase their awareness of the rights of foster children. Typically, this training occurs before they work with foster children. Following this initial training, Foster Parents should keep updated about foster child rights issues.

Fourteen major child rights are introduced in this chapter. These are not all-inclusive, but give a good overview of the training content. For each of these 14 areas there are both rules and guidelines. Certain priorities are called rules because they are rarely modified. Guidelines are less absolute. They serve as guiding principles for Foster Parents, who must exercise discretion and sound judgment. Guidelines are considered to be good practices under most situations. After each youth right and its rules and guidelines are discussed, an example of how Foster Parents might apply that right to promote a safe environment for a child is presented.

# 1. Right to Nourishment

Foster Parents must provide each foster child with healthy food and proper nutrition.

## Rules:

1. Foster Parents must provide three nutritionally sound meals (and nutritious snacks) to the foster child each and every day.
2. The three main meals (breakfast, lunch, and dinner) should never be used as a privilege or withheld as punishment.
3. Meals should never be made intentionally less adequate, less tasty, or less nutritious for any reason.
4. Medical advice and guardian consent should be obtained before starting weight-loss or other "special" dietary programs for foster children.

## Guidelines:

1. Foster Parents should provide a wide variety of nutritious foods for the foster child, including ethnic and religious preferences.

2. Foster Parents should avoid imposing personal food preferences on foster children (e.g., vegetarian or sugar-free diets) or fad diets (e.g., eggs and grapefruit for each meal).

3. While some snacks (e.g., sweet snacks) can be used as a privilege, nutritious snacks such as fruits or vegetables should be made freely available (e.g., apples after school).

4. Junk food (e.g., chips, candy) should be available only in moderation. Totally prohibiting junk food is unreasonable.

## Example:

Michael, age 10, returns home late from a visit with his family. Dinner has been over for several hours and the kitchen has been cleaned up. The Foster Parent tells Michael that there is a plate of food from dinner in the refrigerator for him to heat up and eat.

## 2. Right to Communicate with Significant Others

Foster Parents should actively teach foster children how to appropriately communicate with others. Healthy relationships with significant others are desirable for all foster children.

## Rules:

1. Foster children have a right to seek help or communicate with significant others such as parents, legal guardians, caseworkers, or clergy.

2. Communication with significant others should not be used as a consequence or as a privilege (e.g., because Dante did not apologize to his teacher, he cannot call his mother).

3. Foster Parents should provide methods (mail or phone) for routine and emergency contact with significant others.

4. Foster Parents should advocate for each foster child's right to directly present his or her own case in any formal or informal proceeding.

## Guidelines:

1. Foster Parents can exercise reasonable control over the form, frequency (e.g., two long-distance calls per month), and timing of communication (e.g., allowing a child to call a caseworker when the child is calm).

2. Control over the form, frequency, and timing of communication should not be unreasonable. For example, even though a foster child is not completely calm, he or she can call a legal guardian after there has been a reasonable attempt to calm the child.

## Example:

The foster mother is talking with 15-year-old old Sara, who is angry, yelling, and threatening to run away. Sara demands to call her caseworker right away. The foster mother tries to discourage Sara from calling while she is so angry and to call when she has calmed down.

## 3. Right to Respect of Body and Person

Foster Parents should use interaction styles that are as pleasant as possible and that demonstrate humane, professional, concerned care at all times. Physical contact (e.g., guidance, restraint) is strongly discouraged and should be used only when the foster child is in clear and immediate danger of harming himself or herself or others. (Note: Foster Parents should receive restraint training before they ever restrain a foster child. In addition, Foster Parents should always adhere to the program's policies and procedure regarding restraint.)

### Rules:

1. Corporal (i.e., physical) punishment or threats of corporal punishment should never be used to discipline foster children (e.g., hitting, spanking, unnecessary work, or physical exercise). An example of unnecessary work would be having a child dig a hole and refill it as a consequence for arguing with a Foster Parent.

2. Foster Parents should use restraint only if they have been trained in those techniques. (Note: Restraint should be used as a last option and only when it is necessary to prevent a child from harming himself or herself or others.)

3. Foster Parents should avoid sarcasm, labeling, or name-calling; such practices can humiliate a foster child (e.g., discussing Jordan's bed-wetting with members of the family).

4. The use of curse words, threats, or yelling directed toward the foster child is never appropriate.

## Guidelines:

1. The least possible force should be employed.

## Example:

The foster dad has just told 7-year-old Jose that he can't go next door to his friend's house because he came in late the day before. Jose is yelling, cursing, and walking around. Then he shakes his fist at his Foster Parent and says, *"If you don't let me go, I'll hit you."* The foster father responds by talking with Jose until he has calmed down and is able to accept his consequence. Instead of using restraint, the foster dad gives Jose time to calm down before addressing the issue.

# 4. Right to Have One's Own Possessions

Each foster child has a right to possessions that are in keeping with his or her developmental level and living situation. Foster Parents should respect a foster child's right to possessions and should create a home atmosphere that encourages the foster child to own developmentally appropriate personal possessions. Also, community standards and rules of common decency should be applied to determine if a child's possessions are appropriate. Foster Parents should consult their program supervisor when there are questions concerning the appropriateness of a child's personal possessions.

## Rules:

1. Foster Parents should ensure that foster children do not possess dangerous items (drugs, guns, knives).

2. Foster Parents should ensure that foster children have the necessary materials for school or a job, and that these materials are similar to those of their peers (books, clothes).

3. Foster Parents should never break or permanently take away a foster child's possessions (other than dangerous possessions) unless the foster child waives his or her right to the possession or unless the possession is taken away so that it can be turned over to the foster child's legal guardian. Note: If an item is taken away for an extended period of time (e.g., a month), send it to the youth's guardian. A Foster Parent does not want to be held responsible for an item getting broken or being lost while in his or her possession.

## Guidelines:

1. Foster Parents can exercise reasonable control over the possessions foster children bring into the home (e.g., no illegal or stolen property, no pagers).

2. Foster Parents can limit the use of personal possessions to reasonable times or places (e.g., no stereo played after bedtime).

3. If a foster child is restricted from appropriate use of his or her personal possessions, he or she should

be told how to earn back the use of the possessions.

## Example:

Maria (13-years-old) has a set of stereo headphones that she likes to wear when walking to school. A teacher caught Maria listening to music in study hall. The Foster Parents and Maria discuss and agree that she can no longer wear the headphones to school; however, she still has the use of her headphones in the evening and on the weekends.

## 5. Right to Privacy

Under the right to privacy, Foster Parents should ensure that each foster child has the rights typically given to people in our society. Each foster child should have adequate personal living space and storage areas. Each foster child's right to physical privacy should be protected. (It is important to follow your program's policies and licensing requirements in this area and talk with your supervisor if any questions arise.)

## Rules:

1. Foster Parents should not open a foster child's mail or listen in on phone conversations without the child's permission. If you suspect that a piece of mail contains illegal material, you may ask the child to open the mail in your presence or confiscate the mail and return it unopened to the sender. Foster Parents cannot open a foster child's mail

without signed written permission from the child's legal guardian.

2. Foster Parents should not conduct routine searches of a foster child's room or belongings. A search would be appropriate if you believe a child has something that is dangerous or illegal. (During the search, the youth should be present.)

3. Foster Parents should never search a foster child's body.

4. Foster Parents can release program records only to a foster child's legal guardian or persons who have written permission from a foster child's legal guardian.

## Guidelines:

1. Foster Parents should assure that privacy is available in the foster child's living space and for his or her belongings (bed, dresser, clothes).

## Example:

Twelve-year-old Tracy has been caught smoking cigarettes on several occasions. In an effort to curb Tracy's smoking, her foster mother decides to search Tracy's room for cigarettes after she gets home from school so Tracy can be present.

# 6. Right to Freedom of Movement

Each foster child has a right to a wide range of experiences according to his or her age and maturity level.

Procedures that physically restrict movement or consequences that don't allow exposure to healthy activities for extended periods of time are discouraged.

## Rules:

1. Foster Parents must not use seclusion or isolation as a discipline practice (e.g., child is locked in a room or isolated from the family).
2. A foster child should always be provided with options for earning privileges. This will help keep a child motivated to want to do better.

## Guidelines:

1. Foster Parents can limit a foster child's movements to a given area and time (e.g., in school from 8 a.m. to 4:15 p.m., at home from 4:30 p.m. to 6 p.m.).
2. Time-out is an acceptable procedure for certain children, provided that the Foster Parents have received training and supervision on its use and clearly understand how to carry it out.

## Example:

Alex, a 5-year-old foster child, disrupts dinner by not following instructions, throwing food, and kicking others under the table. His foster father sends Alex to the living room where he can sit for five minutes and calm down. After five minutes, the foster father goes to Alex in the living room to see if he has calmed down and is ready to finish dinner.

# 7. Right Not to Be Given Meaningless Work

Foster Parents should ensure that each foster child lives in an environment where chores, tasks, goals, and privileges are meaningful learning experiences. Ideally, consequences for problem behaviors will have immediate teaching benefits and should not be principally punishing in nature.

## Rules:

1. Foster Parents should never give "make work" tasks (e.g., cleaning a floor with a toothbrush, digging a hole and refilling it, or writing a sentence 200 times).

2. Procedures that are designed solely to punish the foster child should not be used (e.g., having the foster child kneel and hold a broom above his or her head, or eat soap as a consequence for using profanity).

3. Foster children should be paid according to the prevailing wage and hour laws when performing personal work for Foster Parents.

## Guidelines:

1. Foster Parents can assign chores and tasks related to daily living that teach family or personal values (e.g., making one's bed or doing family dishes).

2. Removal from typical responsibilities and activities

(e.g., jobs, athletic teams, clubs, lessons, or church) should not routinely be used as a consequence for problem behaviors. Note: While a foster child sometimes must be removed from these activities, this should be done only when the behavior is so serious that it cancels out the benefit of continued participation. For example, a foster father's first thought is to pull a child off the basketball team because she violated curfew. However, after talking it over with the foster mother, who points out all the benefits (e.g., responsibility, teamwork, time management, making friends) that the foster child has received by being a member of the team, another consequence (a one-hour earlier curfew for two weeks) is given.

## Example:

David, who is 9, has been arguing with his foster sister about many things throughout the day. Finally, the foster mother pulls David aside after she sees him continuing to tease his sister while they are doing the dishes. David's consequence for teasing is to do an extra after-dinner chore (wash the pots and pans).

# 8. Right to Interact with Others

Foster children should be taught skills that enhance their relationships with peers and adults. Foster children should be provided with ample opportunities to interact with peers. Foster Parents should monitor the child's social contacts to ensure that they are appropriate.

### Rules:

1. Isolation should not be used as a consequence for problem behaviors or for any other reason (e.g., instructing other children not to talk to a foster child as a consequence for a problem behavior).

### Guidelines:

1. Foster Parents may limit interactions between foster children and their peers (e.g., foster children with known substance abuse or sexual issues may be limited or supervised more closely in their interactions with peers until these problems are resolved).

2. Foster Parents may limit when and how the foster child interacts with peers (e.g., no wrestling, no playing in bedrooms with doors closed).

### Example:

Mary, age 8, has a problem with cursing. In order to help her overcome this problem, the Foster Parents and Mary agree on a new rule. It states that whenever Mary curses, she loses one hour of time playing outside with the neighborhood kids.

## 9. Right to Basic Clothing Necessities

Foster children should be provided with appropriate dress and leisure clothing in keeping with their age and sex. Foster Parents should ensure that each foster child's basic clothing needs are met at all times.

## Rules:

1. Basic clothing needs should never be used as a negative consequence for problem behavior (e.g., foster child doesn't get a replacement coat as a consequence for losing one).
2. Each foster child has a right to the same style, type, and quantity of clothing that is provided for other foster children in the home.
3. Clothing should meet the needs of seasonal changes and the growth of the child.

## Guidelines:

1. A foster child's preference in clothing should be strongly considered by Foster Parents so long as the personal preference is not extremely deviant in style or overly expensive in price.
2. Foster Parents can limit the style of clothing to be consistent with the goals of an individual foster child (e.g., sexually provocative clothing should not be worn).

## Example:

Roma's Foster Parents take her shopping for clothes. She wants to buy a shirt displaying a musical group that glorifies self-harm and suicide. This is an issue that Roma is working on with a counselor. The foster parents say "No," but allow her to choose a different shirt instead.

## 10. Right to the Natural Elements

Each foster child has a right to natural elements such as fresh air, light, and outdoor exercise. Healthy outdoor activities should be a routine part of every foster child's experience. Foster Parents should ensure that foster children have the opportunity to experience the natural elements each day.

### Rules:

1. Access to the natural elements and indoor light should not be used as a consequence.

### Guidelines:

1. Foster children should be provided with the opportunity for outside activities each day (e.g., walking to and from school or playing in the yard).

2. Foster Parents can regulate the amount of time spent outside, the degree of supervision provided for the foster child, and what activities the child may or may not do (e.g., riding a bike).

3. It is acceptable to reduce the amount of playtime outside as a consequence. If possible, foster children should be given a chance to earn some of this time back by engaging in appropriate behavior.

### Example:

For several days, 6-year-old Russell has not gotten along with other children while playing in the yard. He appears to become very aggressive with the other children when he thinks they are "not playing fair." The foster mother observes Russell pushing a playmate down and decides to take away Russell's privilege of playing outside for two hours. However, Russell can earn some of that time back by practicing with his foster mom how to stay calm when he's angry.

## 11. Right to One's Own Bed

Each foster child has a right to a personal bed and a private sleeping area or room shared with another child of the same sex and similar age.

### Rules:

1. A foster child's access to a personal bed or bedding should never be restricted during normal sleeping hours.

### Guidelines:

1. Foster Parents may have more than one child share a bedroom provided that ample space (according to state licensing guidelines) and privacy are assured, and that the children's past and background are not in conflict.

2. Foster Parents may regulate a foster child's access to his or her bedroom during nonsleeping hours or limit privacy of sleeping arrangements when a foster child is at risk (especially when a foster child is suicidal), or when inappropriate sexual behavior is an issue.

3. Foster Parents may use earlier bedtime as a negative consequence or later bedtime as a positive consequence. In this instance, a reasonable consequence would be one hour earlier or later than a child's normal bedtime.

### Example:

The foster family is having relatives come visit for the holidays. They don't have enough bedrooms for everyone. So, the Foster Parents ask the 12-year-old foster daughter to sleep on a foldout couch in the den and their 10-year-old daughter to sleep on a spare bed set up in their room.

## 12. Right to Visit Family

Each foster child may visit his or her family and receive visits, unless otherwise stated in writing by his or her legal guardian.

### Rules:

1. Foster Parents are expected to help provide or arrange for transportation to and from parental visits, if necessary.

2. Foster children do not have to "earn" visits with their families unless the legal guardian agrees in writing that it is in a foster child's best interest to make visits dependent on the child's behavior.

3. The length or setting of the visit can be modified to provide the type and amount of structure neces-

sary to promote a positive visiting environment for the foster child.

## Guidelines:

1. Foster Parents may host the foster child's visits with his or her family in the foster home if they wish.
2. Foster Parents should support the foster child in developing the best relationship possible with his or her family and extended family.

## Example:

Sherri has been living with a foster family for two weeks when her first home visit is scheduled. The Foster Parents read Sherri's social history prior to her placement, and they were surprised and saddened that she had gone through so much in her young life. The Foster Parents know that home visits are a part of Sherri's getting better. However, when Sherri returns from the home visit, she is argumentative, refuses to eat dinner with the rest of the family, and complains that she is "in prison." The Foster Parents work together with Sherri's mother to develop similar rules so that Sherri's weekly home visits can remain uninterrupted.

# 13. Right to Participate in Care

Youth have a right to participate in planning their own care and to refuse any specific therapy or medication unless those rights have been limited by law or court order.

## Rules:

1. Each foster child is provided care in accordance with his or her reasonable wishes and that of his or her legal guardian.

2. Should the foster child refuse care, he or she will be informed of the consequences, which may include removal from the foster home. The child may be discharged from the home and program if the Foster Parents and program supervisor believe the refusal of care or medication jeopardizes the safety of the foster child or the foster family or is inconsistent with the goals of a community-based placement.

## Guidelines:

1. Foster Parents are encouraged to make reasonable efforts to resolve the foster child's or guardian's concerns regarding questions about care.

2. Foster Parents are expected to be sensitive to cultural and racial issues.

## Example:

Miguel was in a psychiatric hospital prior to moving into a foster home. When he was discharged from the hospital, part of Miguel's care included an order from the court that he begin individual therapy when he moved to the foster home. After living in the foster home for three weeks, he says he is tired of being in therapy and doesn't want to go anymore. Miguel's Foster Parents tell him that this choice might jeopardize his placement in their home and the program.

## 14. Right to Lodge a Complaint or Appeal

Each foster child and his or her parents or legal guardian have the right to express a grievance or complaint.

### Rules:

1. Each foster care program should have its own procedure for filing grievances. The grievance process will vary, depending on that program's protocol. Foster Parents should thoroughly understand their program's protocol.

### Guidelines:

1. Staff and Foster Parents should make every reasonable effort to address and resolve complaints so as to provide the highest level of care possible to the foster child.

2. Reasonable efforts should be made to resolve conflict so that the foster child can experience the fewest disruptions in his or her placement as possible.

### Example:

Terrance, 17, has been in his new foster home for a year. He has been planning a trip to a town three hours away to visit a childhood friend whom he hasn't seen for some time. The trip is scheduled for a Saturday and Sunday and is two weeks away. Terrance has bought a bus ticket for the trip with money he has been saving. His parents and his caseworker have given their permission for him to make the trip. However, the trip is on the same weekend that his Foster Parents want to take the family camping. Terrance's Foster Parents listen to his appeal and agree to delay the family camping trip until he gets back because they believe the outing would be a good chance for the foster family to spend time together.

# Additional Standards

Following are some additional areas where Foster Parents should be aware of maintaining professional standards.

## Consequences

Foster Parents should not use or engage in the following:

1. Severe consequences, such as having a foster child sit in the car while the rest of the family participates in an outing.
2. Taking away money that a foster child has earned as a consequence.

## Modeling

The following is a list of examples of inappropriate modeling by Foster Parents:

1. Inappropriate teasing or humiliation of a foster child (e.g., racial slurs or put-downs based on religion, background, or parents). This also includes sexual harassment.
2. Indiscreet or excessive use of alcohol; DWI violations.
3. Use of illegal drugs.
4. Swearing at foster children or other family members.
5. Showing movies with sexually provocative or violent scenes to foster children, or allowing them access to such movies (e.g., having X-rated videos in the home). Note: Any video shown in the home should be age appropriate for the youth viewing it.
6. Indiscreet display of sexual behaviors in front of foster children, including pinching, prolonged kissing, inappropriate dress by parents, or extra-marital affairs.
7. Verbal aggression toward consumers, including becoming visibly upset in public (e.g., yelling or cursing at parents, teachers, or store clerks).

## Coercion

Examples of coercing or intimidating a foster child into doing something include:

1. Offering bribes of money or other rewards to a foster child for providing positive responses to questions from parents or others about the Foster

Parents (or threatening to harm the child for negative responses).

2. Telling a foster child what to tell or not tell his or her parents or the youth's caseworker.

3. Asking a child to do something illegal or unethical.

## Neglect

The following are examples of neglect of a foster child's basic care:

1. Neglecting a foster child's medical care. Examples include failing to give a foster child medication, improperly giving medication, and failing to get the foster child to a doctor, dentist, or other scheduled appointment.

2. Serving nutritionally inadequate meals. Examples of this include poorly prepared meals, nutritionally poor foods, or lack of variety (e.g., always serving only hot dogs, frozen pizza).

3. Failure to report dangerous behavior (e.g., suicide statements, ideations, or gestures).

4. Failure to adequately monitor the foster child. For example, allowing a 10-year-old foster child to stay out until midnight.

## Abuse

The following are examples of abuse of a foster child:

1. Using physical restraints. On rare occasions, in strict compliance with the program's policies on restraint, the Foster Parent may need to physically

assist a foster child who is a danger to himself or herself, or others. If the child is hurt, Foster Parents must immediately report the use of restraint to a supervisor or the person designated in the program's protocol.

2. Slapping, pushing, shoving, grabbing, punching, hitting, or throwing objects at a foster child with the intent to hurt him or her.

## Professionalism

The following are examples of a lack of professionalism:

1. Failing to report serious incidents, including incidents involving restraint, regarding the foster child.

2. Refusing to cooperate or being dishonest with the agency.

3. Serious or consistent refusal to accept or implement feedback.

4. Mismanaging a foster child's money.

5. Violating confidentiality.

6. Intentionally risky or unsafe driving with a foster child.

7. Lack of advocacy for the program.

## Religion

The following are examples of inappropriate behaviors regarding religious activities:

1. Failing to take a foster child to church and/or restricting his or her religious beliefs.
2. Proselytizing (i.e., trying to convert a child to your own religious faith) or making inappropriate or critical statements about a foster child's beliefs or religion.
3. Forcing a foster child to participate or denying his or her right to participate in Bible studies or religious discussions.
4. Repeatedly showing religious videos or playing religious music while excluding other forms of entertainment.
5. Overusing God or religion as a rationale for why certain behavior is okay or not okay.

## Sexual Behavior

The following are examples of inappropriate sexual behaviors with or around youth:

1. Inappropriate affection toward a foster child, including dating a current or former foster child, or inappropriate touching of the foster child.
2. Talking with a foster child about inappropriate sexual issues, including telling a child about personal sexual experiences or insisting that a foster child talk about his or her past sexual feelings or behaviors.
3. Taking a foster child into the Foster Parents' bedroom. (Follow your agency's protocols and use

common sense about whether a child should be allowed to enter a Foster Parent's bedroom.) Foster Parents should avoid even the appearance of impropriety. Foster Parents must remember that in some cases, foster children may have been abused in their parents' bedroom.

4. Reinforcing adolescent infatuation. This might include giving a child jewelry (necklaces, rings), attempting to maintain a "special" relationship with a foster child who has left the foster home (a relationship that excludes a spouse), or encouraging a foster child to rely exclusively on the Foster Parents to the extent that he or she is discouraged from seeking help from others.

5. Allowing inappropriate sexual activities between a foster child and another child or adult.

## When a Child's Rights Are Violated

Foster care programs should look into any questionable practice reported by a foster child or a Foster Parent. At Girls and Boys Town, we use a formal Child Rights Violation Inquiry to obtain the facts about any questionable practice. Inquiries are investigations into suspected or alleged inappropriate practices reported by a foster child or a consumer, or observed by a supervisor or another Foster Parent. (Girls and Boys Town foster care programs investigate all reports, regardless of their perceived validity or seriousness. Even relatively minor allegations are investigated to address potential problems early when they can be most easily solved.)

As a Foster Parent, you are responsible for safeguarding the rights of foster children. Any suspected abuse of a youth's rights by a Foster Parent or another person (e.g., teacher, employer) should immediately be reported to your program supervisor. This way, facts can be established and conclusions can be reached as quickly as possible. And, any danger or discomfort experienced by a foster child and/or any harm to a Foster Parent's reputation can be dispelled in a timely manner.

## Summary

Ensuring that each foster child's rights are respected comes not only from following procedures, but also from the "sense of quality" that is instilled in each Foster Parent. Each Foster Parent's competence in carrying out quality care and continually monitoring his or her own actions and the actions of others make the real difference. Rules, guidelines, and procedures are necessary, but it is the commitment to providing the highest quality care possible that guarantees each foster child a safe environment.

# CHAPTER 5

# Setting Expectations and Sending Clear Messages

*"Nice job!"*

*"You've got a lousy attitude!"*

*"Shape up! Stop being so naughty."*

*"You were a good boy at the store."*

Parents and Foster Parents commonly make these kinds of statements to their children. But do children really understand what they mean? For most, the answer is "No." Kids are concrete thinkers; they don't grasp the full meaning of words that are abstract or vague. Telling a child he is "a good boy" or that he has "a lousy attitude" does not give him enough information to know what he did right or what he needs to change. Clearer messages might be, *"You took out the garbage without being asked"* or *"You walked away from me when I asked you to load the dishwasher, and mumbled, 'Do it yourself.'"* Using these kinds of statements gives children specific information about their behavior that they can understand and act on.

Giving clear messages is one key to effective discipline. As a Foster Parent, you should specifically tell your foster children what needs to be done and how to do it. You should tell them when they've done something well, correct them when they mess up, and help them learn from their mistakes. Finally, you should teach foster children how to think for themselves, solve problems, and set goals.

But before this can happen, Foster Parents must know and learn how to communicate clearly. They must be specific, focus on what the child is doing or saying, and describe his or her behaviors. Everyone has a general idea of what behaviors are. But, to make sure we're on the same page, let's take a look at a common sense definition that can help Foster Parents give clear messages.

## Describing Behaviors

**Behavior is what people do or say. It is an action that can be seen, heard, or measured.** The following is a descriptive list of behaviors:

- *"My foster child sets the table for dinner without being asked."*
- *"My foster child talks on the phone for one hour at a time."*
- *"When I ask my foster son to do something, he rolls his eyes and walks away."*
- *"When my foster children come home from school, they put their books away and ask if there's anything that needs to be done around the house."*

- *"When I tell my foster daughter her jeans are too tight, she whines and complains, saying, 'But everyone else wears them.'"*
- *"My foster son helped me put away the dishes. Then he swept the kitchen floor."*

It is easy to understand what we mean by actions that can be seen or heard. You *see* your foster child throw a toy. You *hear* your foster child singing to her baby sister. But what do we mean by *measuring* a behavior? Think of it this way: You can measure how long a person lies on a couch by the length of time that passes. Lying on the couch is a behavior; it's something a person does. But you can't measure how long a person has been "lazy." Laziness is a perception; it is an interpretation and is not behaviorally specific.

Terms such as "hyperactive," "naughty," or "irresponsible" are far from clear, concrete descriptions. These words describe perceptions; people see or hear something and form mental impressions of another person. Perceptions are formed from observing a person's behavior. The problem is that when these perceptions are conveyed to others, they can easily be misunderstood and can mean different things to different people. For example, "irresponsible" may mean not coming home on time or leaving the kitchen a mess to one Foster Parent. To another Foster Parent, "irresponsible" may mean not helping

> Giving clear messages is one key to effective discipline.

around the house or not putting the lawn mower away. To give clear messages, Foster Parents must describe *behaviors,* not give perceptions.

## How to Give Clear Messages

Have you ever listened to a sporting event on the radio? If you have, you know that a good sports announcer enables you to visualize what is happening through his descriptions. He gives a verbal replay of the action taking place, and you can see every play in your mind. As a Foster Parent, you must be just as clear with foster children.

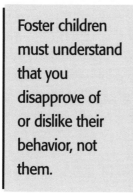

**Foster children must understand that you disapprove of or dislike their behavior, not them.**

To give clear messages, watch what a child says or does. Then, clearly and specifically tell the child what he or she did or did not do. Use words that you know the child will understand. For younger children, use short sentences and small words. As kids get older, adjust your language to fit their age and level of comprehension.

The following are some questions you can ask yourself that will help you to give clear descriptions:

- **Who** is involved, who is being praised, and whose behavior is being corrected?

- **What** just happened, what was done well, what needs to be improved or changed?

- **When** does the behavior occur?
- **Where** does the behavior occur?

How you express the description of your foster child's behavior also is very important. Here are several points that will help you give clear messages and expectations to your foster child:

**Have your foster child look at you.**

It's more likely that he or she will hear what you say and follow through on any requests. Our experience has taught us that eye contact is a key to giving and receiving clear messages.

**Look at your foster child.**

This shows that you are paying attention and allows you to see his or her reaction to what you say. Give your foster child your full attention.

**Use a voice tone that fits the situation.**

Your voice should be firm when giving correction, friendly when giving compliments, and so on.

**Be aware of your facial expressions and body language.**

For example, you might smile when you are happy about something your foster child has done or frown when you are displeased.

**Eliminate as many distractions as possible.**

Try to find a quiet area where you can talk to your foster child.

**Position yourself so that you are at eye level with your foster child.**

Avoid intimidating the child by standing over him or her.

One important thing to keep in mind about clear messages: The most important part of being specific when describing your foster children's misbehavior is that they understand that you disapprove of or dislike their *behavior, not them.* You must convey that you are upset and displeased with the way they are acting, but you still care for them; that's why you are taking the time to teach them another way to behave.

Let's take a look at some examples of clear and unclear messages.

- *"Jamel, why can't you act your age when company comes?"* (Unclear message)
- *"When we get to the store, please be a nice girl."* (Unclear message)
- *"Jaime, would you please rake the backyard, put the leaves in a big plastic bag, and put the bag on the front curb?"* (Clear message)
- *"That was a nice story you wrote for English class, Sam."* (Unclear message)
- *"Sadie, you need to stop talking right now."* (Clear message)
- *"Reggie, don't eat like a pig."* (Unclear message)
- *"Veronica, when you chew your food, you should keep your mouth closed."* (Clear message)

- *"Connor, after school you are to come right home. Don't stop to play."* (Clear message)
- *"Roberto, thank you for sitting still and not talking in church."* (Clear message)

Now, let's change the vague statements from the previous list into clear messages:

- *"Jamel, you're whining about your sister taking your toy. I'd like you to go to the family room and politely ask her to give it back."*
- *"When we get to the store, remember that we aren't buying any candy. Okay? I'd like you to help me pick out the things on our list and put them in the cart. You can push the shopping cart. Okay?"*
- *"Sam, you did a nice job on that story for English class. You used complete sentences and all of the grammar was correct. The topic of prejudice was excellent! It was really interesting."*
- *"Reggie, you're eating with your fingers and making grunting noises while you eat. I'd like you to eat with a fork, take small bites, and not make any noises."*

These statements include descriptions of what each foster child said or did. When a child's behaviors are described this way, the child is more likely to understand what needs to be changed.

## Framework for Giving Clear Messages

You may have noticed that most of the clear messages just listed follow a general pattern. There's a reason for that: Using a framework consistently really helps Foster Parents to give clear messages. This framework has two parts that work well for both praising behavior and correcting behavior.

### Framework for Praising Behavior

1. **Show your approval.** Start by saying something like, *"You really did a nice job with..."* or *"Thanks for..."* or *"That's fantastic! You...."*

2. **Describe what was done well.** *"...sweeping and mopping the floor,"* or *"...playing quietly with your sister,"* or *"...studying hard all week and getting a 'B' on your test."*

Sometimes, you can praise behavior in one sentence; for example, *"Thanks for taking the shovel back to Mr. Jones."* This may sound very basic, but it is extremely important that your foster child hears your approval and knows exactly what was done right. Remember to give clear, positive messages!

### Examples

**Show your approval:** *"You really did a great job!"*

**Describe what was done well:** *"You put in a lot of time and effort studying for your math test."*

**Show your approval:** *"Thanks for helping out."*

**Describe what was done well:** *"You took the time to help me make a grocery list and cut out the coupons. I really appreciate it."*

**Show your approval:** *"Awesome catch!"*

**Describe what was done well:** *"You stayed right in front of the ball and kept your eye on it. It was really hit hard!"*

**Show your approval:** *"Wow! You're downstairs already!"*

**Describe what was done well:** *"You set the alarm clock last night and got up on your own. That's three days in a row!"*

**Show your approval:** *"You did a fantastic job on this English paper."*

**Describe what was done well:** *"You wrote the paper neatly; you used proper grammar, and you expressed your ideas clearly."*

## Framework for Correcting Behavior

1. **Describe what happened.** Tell your foster child exactly what needs to be changed or stopped. Start by saying something like, *"What you're doing now is..."* or *"You did..."* or *"You said...."*

2. **Describe what you want done.** Your foster child needs to know specifically what you expect of him or her. Begin by saying something like, *"What I'd like you to do is..."* or *"Please go and...."*

## Examples

**Describe what happened:** *"Thomas, you left the milk out on the counter, and there are potato chip crumbs on the floor."*

**Describe what you want done:** *"Please go out to the kitchen and put the milk in the refrigerator. Then sweep the floor and throw the crumbs in the trash."*

**Describe what happened:** *"Mrs. Johnson called and said that on your way home, you rode your bike through her flowers."*

**Describe what you want done:** *"We are going to go back over to her house, and you'll need to tell her you are sorry. Then ask her if you can do anything to make up for riding your bike through her flowers."*

**Describe what happened:** *"Sandy, your music is too loud."*

**Describe what you want done:** *"Please turn it down and shut your door."*

**Describe what happened:** *"Right now you are arguing with me."*

**Describe what you want done:** *"I'd appreciate it if you would be quiet and let me finish talking. Then you can have your turn to speak. Okay?"*

## Situations

The following situations point out the differences between giving clear messages and making vague comments.

**Situation:** Your two foster children are arguing about who had a toy first.

**Vague:** *"Cut that out!"*

**Specific:** *"You two are arguing with me about who had the toy first. Please give me the toy and sit quietly."*

**Situation:** Your 4-year-old foster child is using his spoon to eat his food.

**Vague:** *"You're being such a good boy."*

**Specific:** *"All right! I'm so happy. You're using your spoon to eat! You're keeping all of the food on the spoon. Good job!"*

**Situation:** Your teenage foster daughter slams her books on the kitchen table.

**Vague:** *"What do you think you're doing?"*

**Specific:** *"I understand that you're frustrated because you wanted to keep playing outside. But when you came in to study, you slammed your books on the table."*

**Situation:** Your 17-year-old foster son spends 45 minutes on his homework instead of talking on the phone.

**Vague:** *"Gee, what got into you?"*

**Specific:** *"Wow! You've really been trying hard to get your grades up. Sitting here quietly studying for 45 minutes instead of talking on the phone will help you reach your goal. I'm really proud of you!"*

## Summary

Try these methods for giving clear messages and setting expectations at home with your children and/or foster children. Watch what they do and say for the next day or two. When you praise or correct them, use the frameworks discussed in this chapter. If you focus on describing what your foster child does or says, you'll send clear messages. This is the first step toward helping your foster kids understand what you expect from them and more effective Foster Parenting.

# CHAPTER 6

# The Benefits of Teaching

Some foster children who come to your home may have much to learn and unlearn in a relatively short time. They may have problems with controlling their anger or not doing what you or other adults ask them to do. They may have tried to run away, failed in school, or used alcohol, drugs, or sex to forget their problems. One of the main reasons for these types of behaviors is that the children have not been taught or have not learned appropriate behaviors or how to respond to difficult situations. That is why *frequent, specific,* and *skillful teaching* is so important in providing safe and effective foster care.

So what do you teach? The answer is social skills. Teaching social skills is one of the hallmarks of Girls and Boys Town's foster care model. Our research has shown that teaching skills, combined with compassion and love, can produce positive changes in children's behavior (Mott, Authier, Shannon, Arneil, & Daly, 1995). When kids know when and how to use social skills, they are more likely to make good choices about their behavior and how they respond to the world around them. They also have a set of positive behaviors to use in place of the negative behaviors they might have used in the past to get their needs met. By focusing on teaching social skills, Foster Parents help children learn to continue their positive behaviors, successfully and comfortably adapt to society's expectations, and get their needs met in socially acceptable ways. (We'll discuss the kinds of social skills to teach in the next chapter.)

**The best way to discipline children is to give them new behaviors, along with consequences, when they misbehave.**

Specific, frequent, and skillful teaching also helps Foster Parents. Teaching is a safe, effective, and positive way to deal with problem behaviors that might arise. Because teaching is a positive approach that works well and is liked by foster children, Foster Parents can steer away from methods that might physically or emotionally harm kids and, inevitably, damage relationships. Oftentimes, parents and Foster Parents immediately turn to punishment when dealing with a child's misbehavior. While punishment might let children know what they did *wrong,* it doesn't teach them the *right* thing to do. For this reason, we believe that the best way to discipline children is to give them new behaviors (skills), along with consequences, when they misbehave. We have developed two methods – *Corrective*

*Teaching* and *Teaching Self-Control* – that enable Foster Parents to deal with these situations. (See the box on page 110.) The style of teaching we advocate does both.

So far, we have discussed how teaching is used to deal with problem behaviors. It is equally important to remember that teaching also can be used to praise and reinforce children's positive behaviors. By identifying the strengths children bring with them into a home, teaching kids skills before they need to use them, and praising kids when they do good things, Foster Parents set the stage for real progress. To accomplish these goals, Foster Parents use *Proactive Teaching* and *Effective Praise.* (See page 110.) When children begin to understand that there are some behaviors they should continue to use and others they should change, they become more open and receptive to the teaching Foster Parents offer.

Before we discuss how you can make your teaching more effective, it is important to understand the differences between discipline and punishment. The next section outlines those differences and explains how to recognize them. It also explains why adults often react to a child's misbehavior in an emotional, negative, punishing manner, rather than in a calm, positive, constructive way.

## Punishment or Discipline?

**Punishment:** "...suffering, pain, or loss that serves as retribution ...a penalty inflicted on an offender through judicial procedure ...severe, rough, or disastrous treatment." *New World College Dictionary (1997)*

## Teaching Interactions and Steps

### Proactive Teaching

1. Describe the skill or behavior.
2. Give a reason.
3. Practice.

### Effective Praise

1. Show your approval.
2. Describe the positive behavior/Label the skill.
3. Give a reason.
4. (Optional) Give a reward.

### Corrective Teaching

1. Stop the problem behavior.
2. Deliver a consequence.
3. Describe what your foster child could do differently next time/Label the skill.
4. Give a reason.
5. Practice what your foster child could do differently next time.

### Teaching Self-Control

*Part 1: Calming Down*

1. Describe the problem behavior.
2. Give clear instructions.
3. Allow time to calm down.

*Part 2: Corrective Teaching*

1. Describe what your foster child could do differently next time.
2. Give a reason.
3. Practice what your foster child could do differently next time.
4. Deliver a consequence.

*Part 3: Follow-Up Teaching*

1. Do Proactive Teaching later in the day to ensure that the original issue has been addressed.
2. Teach and practice skills that may be used to prevent future "blow ups."

*(Note: All these teaching interactions will be discussed in detail in later chapters.)*

**Discipline:** "…instruction …training that corrects, molds, or perfects …orderly or prescribed conduct or pattern of behavior…." *New World College Dictionary (1997)*

After reading these two definitions, it should be clear that discipline fits the positive teaching approach of the Girls and Boys Town foster care model much better than punishment. This is not to say that disciplining the children in your care will always be easy. Kids may argue, fight, talk back, throw toys, rip apart books, and curse at you. These can be painful times, and it can be tempting to want to strike back at a child, either verbally or physically, in order to "teach him or her a lesson." But punishing a child with words or actions does not teach anyone a lesson. It only creates resentment and bad feelings, and it damages the relationship you have with the child. And again, most importantly, punishment doesn't tell the child what he or she should do differently next time. In short, Foster Parents must model self-control and provide discipline; punishment is not an option.

Discipline is often misunderstood. The dictionary defines discipline as teaching, instruction, and training. Some people might say, "That's fine, but shouldn't a child have to "pay a price" for misbehavior?" The answer is "Yes." That's where negative consequences come in. These consequences are the part of teaching where a child loses something he or she likes or earns something he or she doesn't like as a result of his or her behavior. A consequence is what happens after, and as a result of, a behavior. Consequences should be used to teach, not punish. Once kids learn that the behaviors they choose to use can lead to consequences – either good or bad – they begin to understand that they have control over what happens to them. This is a big step toward helping kids learn self-discipline.

Discipline doesn't mean letting children get away with misbehavior. In fact, the opposite is true. In order to provide discipline and help children learn new skills, it is important for Foster Parents to identify every misbehavior as an opportunity to teach. Consistently teaching and helping children see the connection between their actions and consequences is the real key to helping kids get better.

In order to determine whether you currently are using discipline or punishment with your children or foster children, please take a moment to read and answer the following questions:

1. Do you find yourself arguing with your children or foster children?

2. Do you feel like you're always correcting your children or foster children?

3. Do you often get your child or foster child to promise that he or she won't do something again?

4. Do you sometimes respond with a big punishment for a relatively minor misbehavior?

5. Do you sometimes threaten action that you know you won't carry out?

6. Do you find yourself saying things to your child or foster child that you later regret saying?

7. Do you repeat instructions time and time again?

8. Do you often give in to your child's or foster child's demands?

9. Do you find that the more you punish, the more your child or foster child misbehaves?

If your answers to most of these questions are "Yes," you're definitely using punishment. If your answers to two or more of these questions are "Yes," you're using some methods of punishment.

> Consequences should be used to teach, not punish.

We define punishment as something that is harsh and unreasonable, violent, or harmful. Obviously, this includes any kind of corporal punishment. When adults punish by hitting, slapping, or punching, children are hurt emotionally as well as physically. In most states, Foster Parents are forbidden to use corporal punishment with foster children. And even if a state allows it, Foster Parents who use the Girls and Boys Town foster care program are expected not to use these procedures, simply because they violate the rights of children in foster care and do nothing to teach children what they need to do differently.

**In Girls and Boys Town programs, corporal punishment is never allowed.**

Other types of punishments like yelling, belittling, ridiculing, or isolating a foster child also are harmful to a child's healthy development and should not be used, especially with foster children. Foster Parents also are reminded that they can be held legally accountable for injuries to a foster child that result from punishment.

With all its drawbacks, why do adults use punishment with children so often?

First, punishment appears to bring about an immediate change in behavior. Sometimes, this change even lasts for a while. For example, the first few times a parent yells at a child, the child stops what she's doing and becomes quiet. Yelling works, right? Wrong. In the short run, punishment accomplishes what the parent wants. Over time, however, children stop responding to yelling and the adult has to "up the ante" (yell louder or spank) to get the child's attention.

Second, many adults don't know what else to do. Punishment is the only tool they have to let kids know they've done something wrong. When angry or frustrated, many adults, including well-intentioned parents and Foster Parents, can react without thinking; over time, their response becomes automatic. Oftentimes, such reaction leads to hitting, yelling, spanking, or other hurtful punishments. When adults learn to take the time to think about what they can do differently to handle difficult and frustrating situations, they often come up with much better and more humane options.

Third, many adults fear that they'll lose their authority or respect if they don't punish children when they misbehave. These folks think that if they aren't tough enough, the children will be in control. Handing out harsh punishments is the only way these adults know how to show kids

## Negative Effects of Punishment on Children

- **Punishment damages relationships between adults and children.** Over time, your foster children will tend to avoid you if rely on punishment. When this happens, children miss opportunities to learn about values and important social or problem-solving skills.

- **Punishment often leads to revenge.** Typically, children want to get back at a person who punishes them. Many foster children resent being taken from their natural homes, and they miss their parents. When they feel unfairly punished in a foster home, they are less likely to want to stay there. They may not care if their revenge gets them removed from the foster home.

- **Punishment can have a snowball effect.** If one punishment doesn't work, people often try a harsher one; a person's response can escalate from requests to commands, yelling, and even hitting. This type of parenting is not consistent with the goals of foster care and is destructive to a Foster Parent-foster child relationship.

- **Many children in foster care have been verbally and physically abused in the past.** It's important for you to monitor and be aware of behavior that the child might be sensitive to. If a foster child interprets your behavior as similar to a former caretaker's abusive behaviors, it's likely that negative feelings will come flooding back to the child.

that they "mean business." This only leads to more abusive kinds of punishment and, often, more misbehavior.

Finally, many adults resort to punishment because they've never been taught any other way to discipline children. They learned from their parents, who learned from their parents, and on it goes. There's nothing wrong with that; we all learn from our parents. But there are good ways and bad ways to parent; physically or emotionally punishing a child is not a good way. Being open to positive parenting techniques, like teaching, can help Foster Parents avoid the mistakes that others might have made in the past, and help them improve the care they provide for kids.

## Teaching Basics

Using teaching and discipline rather than pain and punishment when dealing with problem behaviors provide a positive environment for foster children. We will discuss teaching techniques and the importance of effective teaching in more detail later in this book. For now, let's discuss some basic components that all Foster Parents should adopt as they begin to rely on teaching as one of their main parenting tools.

**Be positive.**

Notice when your foster children do good things and make good choices, and praise them. Focus on catching kids using positive behaviors more often than you correct misbehavior. Kids thrive on positive attention and they are more likely to try to use appropriate behavior if you acknowledge and praise it.

**Be specific.**

Let your foster children know exactly what they do right or wrong.

**Be clear.**

Help your foster children understand the relationship between what they do and what happens as a result of their actions. Do this by giving kids rationales, or reasons, for why they should continue to use a positive behavior or change a negative behavior. This helps build stronger relationships because your foster child will likely see your corrections as helpful and meaningful.

**Be concrete.**

Give your foster children clear examples of how to improve.

**Be encouraging.**

Help your foster children learn self-discipline, so that they can control their actions and expressions of emotion.

**Be interactive.**

Give your foster children a chance to show what they have learned. Help them practice new skills. Take an active part in the learning process as you and your foster children work together toward a common goal.

**Be informative.**

Be a teacher and a coach, giving information that helps your foster children learn to solve problems.

Incorporating these things into your teaching helps foster children to develop self-confidence, get along well with others, and learn the skills they need to make their own decisions.

Foster Parents who take a teaching approach to caring for kids rely on guidance rather than control. An important goal in teaching is helping kids to learn to behave a certain way because it's the right thing to do. If children start using new skills and behaviors only to avoid being punished, the teaching is missing its mark. Foster children are much more likely to learn when they are treated with affection and pleasantness than when they are treated with anger and physical punishment. Teaching provides the framework for necessary learning.

A teaching approach also helps foster children learn self-discipline and self-control, two very important skills for children to master if they are to be successful in life. A teaching approach helps foster children understand what they did right and why they should continue it, or what they did wrong and how to correct it. If you are pleasant, firm, consistent, and able to give clear messages, your teaching will be effective.

To wrap up this chapter, here are some examples of how first, punishment and then, teaching might be used by Foster Parents with their foster children. As you read them, think about the teaching concepts that were discussed earlier and how they apply in the teaching examples and how they might be applied instead in the punishment examples.

## Punishment Examples

Miguel is playing a TV video game. John doesn't want to wait his turn, so he walks up and unplugs the game. Miguel hits John with a Ping-Pong paddle. The foster mom hears what's going on, grabs Miguel, shakes him, and says, *"Don't be so hard to get along with!"*

Felicia draws a picture on the living room wall with a red crayon. She finds her foster mom, shows her the picture, and asks her if she likes it. The foster mom spanks Felicia and sends her to her room for an hour.

## Teaching Examples

The foster father tells Ty that he can't go outside to shoot baskets because he has homework to finish. Ty gets angry, stomps his feet, and complains that the foster father is being unfair. The foster father tells Ty that they need to talk about his behavior. First, he tells the boy that he needs to calm down and stop yelling. Moments later, after Ty has settled down, the foster father explains to Ty why learning how to accept "No" for an answer is important and helps him practice how to do it better.

Shante and her friend walk into the living room. They are talking about the new girl in school. Shante's foster mom overhears Shante tell her friend that they shouldn't play with the new girl any more because she doesn't wear stylish clothes. The foster mother asks the girls to sit down, and they talk about how clothes shouldn't determine how someone feels about another person. The foster mother says it is what's inside a person that is important, not what's on the outside.

## Summary

The key to becoming an effective Foster Parent is teaching your foster children better ways of behaving and interacting with others. The first step in doing this is to focus your attention on a child's positive behavior, acknowledge it, and reward it. Kids are much more likely to continue this kind of behavior in the future. While punishment may seem to be a useful teaching tool initially, in the long run it doesn't teach children better ways of doing things. Remember: Teaching means catching kids being good and correcting misbehavior through guidance. Kids respond positively to this kind of approach.

# CHAPTER 7

# Introduction to Teaching Social Skills

Children and adolescents, like all human beings, are part of social groups. They depend on relationships with others to meet even their most basic needs. A child's sense of well-being is directly related to his or her success, or lack of success, in dealing with significant others. Early in life, young people learn that there are consequences, both positive and negative, attached to how they interact with others and how they choose to respond in social situations. This process of "socialization" begins in the earliest interactions between infant and parent; it prepares kids for more difficult situations later in childhood and through the teenage years. Ideally, lessons learned at each stage in a child's development become the tools he or she uses to successfully meet the challenges presented at later stages of life.

Today, young people face an increasingly difficult world. Many factors can affect a child's ability to learn new skills and change behaviors. Age, developmental level, family problems, substance abuse, economic pressures, the lure of gangs, delinquency, and many other external issues threaten children physically, emotionally, and spiritually. Also, internal issues like possible chemical imbalances in a child's brain, genetic traits inherited from a child's parents, medical problems, and others can have an impact on learning and behavior. In addition, Foster Parents must consider a child's thoughts and feelings – the way a child looks at the world – which have been shaped by his or her past experiences. All these things should be taken into account when caring for kids.

Girls and Boys Town believes that children in foster care have learned or have been taught, often unwittingly, to use the same problem-solving skills that others in their environment (parents, other adults, caregivers, siblings, friends) have used. For example, a child might learn that yelling, screaming, or hitting are ways to solve a problem because he or she sees others do this and get their way. Most youngsters who use these kinds of behaviors haven't had the opportunity to learn more positive ways of coping with problems. Simply put, these children just don't know any other way to handle difficult, frustrating, or upsetting situations.

In order to successfully cope with these external and internal issues, young people must learn how to interact with others in socially acceptable ways and make appropriate decisions in social situations. We believe that this can be done through teaching children social skills. This chapter focuses on social skill instruction and its importance in learning and changing behavior. The social skills presented in this chapter, as well as the techniques described for teaching these skills, have been used successfully for more than 25 years as part of the Girls and Boys Town Teaching Model.

## What Are Social Skills?

Social skills are defined as "the ability to interact with others in specific ways that are socially acceptable and, at the same time, personally or mutually beneficial" (adapted from Combs & Slaby, 1977). This means that social skills help us all function within the rules of our community and society. Parents teach their children social skills when they talk to them about how to be a good student, a good friend, or a good employee. That's how people learn what they need to do to get along with others in their family or community.

While the basic elements of a social skill usually remain constant, how a skill is used may vary from situation to situation and child to child. For instance, you would not greet the mayor of your community in the same way you would greet an old friend. With the mayor, you would show more formal respect. If you greeted your friend that way, he or she probably would think you were joking around. This is one example of how social skills can be adjusted to fit a situation.

Every child is different and develops physically, cognitively, and emotionally at different rates. This means, for example, that a younger child might be developmentally ready to learn a certain higher-level skill (e.g., *Disagreeing Appropriately*) before an older youngster is ready. It's up to you to assess your foster child's learning capabilities and to adjust your teaching to meet his or her needs.

## Why Emphasize Social Skill Teaching?

Many of the children Foster Parents care for have not received the informal social skills training that other kids receive from their parents and teachers. For example, a foster child may appear very uncomfortable and awkward when meeting new people. Or, if you give a new foster child a compliment, he may look away and mumble something sarcastic like, *"Oh, yeah, right."* Even more troubling is the fact that foster children frequently have difficulty using essential social skills like *Following Instructions*. When asked to do something by an adult – a teacher, parent, police officer, or other authority figure – these children may argue, complain, or simply refuse to comply. These types of responses usually lead to problems, and some kind of negative consequence(s), for the children.

In fact, the link between poor social skills and other problems is clear. Children with social skill deficits experience a variety of problems, including aggressive and antisocial behavior, juvenile delinquency, learning problems and school failure, mental health disorders, and loneliness and despondency (Gresham, 1981). Research also indicates that if social and behavioral deficits are not corrected in childhood, they frequently carry over into adulthood (Steinberg & Knitzer, 1992). Without appropriate opportunities to learn better social skills, children fail to correct the deficits on their own (Stephens, 1978). It is easy to see why teaching social skills is very valuable to any child.

**Children with social skill deficits experience a variety of problems, including aggressive and antisocial behavior.**

As a Foster Parent, one of your most important responsibilities is to directly and clearly teach foster children how to use appropriate social skills. Sometimes, this goal must be reached in a short period of time. Many foster children may be in your home only a few months before they return to their family or are placed in a more permanent home. By teaching social skills in a planned, clear way, you can help a child learn many skills in a short period of time. Foster Parents can make this learning process easier by adjusting their techniques, vocabulary, and behaviors to mesh with the foster child's learning style and abilities. Teaching social skills to foster children cannot be overemphasized; it allows them to learn and understand what appropriate behavior is and gives them meaningful behaviors to use in place of inappropriate behaviors. By teaching foster children new social skills, you are really teaching them a new and better way of living.

## Social Skill Components

We defined social skills as "the ability to interact with others in specific ways that are socially acceptable." This means being able to perform a series of behaviors, not just one. When teaching social skills, you will be helping kids learn several behaviors or components that make up each skill. Simply put, teaching social skills is providing your foster child with a specific step-by-step approach to accomplish something. There are four steps to this process (adapted from Cartledge & Milburn, 1980):

1. Describe the skill by identifying what should be accomplished.
2. Identify the essential steps (behaviors) of the goal or skill.
3. State the skill's steps in terms the child understands.
4. List the steps in the order they are to be done.

The following example shows the individual steps you would explain to teach the skill of *Following Instructions*. You might say to a foster child, *"To follow instructions, you should do the following:"*

1. Look at the person who is talking.
2. Show that you understand by saying *'I understand,' 'Okay,'* or *'I'll do it.'* Sometimes nodding your head will be enough.
3. Do what is asked in the best way you can.

4. Let the person know that you have finished.

There are, however, kids who are too young or who might not be developmentally ready to understand and put a series of steps together. In these instances, be flexible when teaching skills and the steps. For example, with younger children or those who are developmentally delayed, you might only teach the first step to *Following Instructions* instead of all four steps at once. Take your time and help the child learn each step until he or she is able to put all four steps together. Remember: assess your child's needs and abilities and adjust your teaching to best match the child's learning capabilities.

## Skills for Children and Teens

Here is a list of the most common skills taught by Foster Parents. The steps to these skills and possible reasons to give a child for why using a skill is important (giving reasons will be discussed in more detail later in the book) are presented in the following section. (Girls and Boys Town has identified and outlined 182 social skills. These skills and the steps to each one are presented in the book, *Teaching Social Skills to Youth,* published by Boys Town Press. Also see the Boys Town Press book, *Treating Youth with DSM-IV Disorders: The Role of Social Skill Instruction.* This book contains a series of charts that list social skills to teach to children and adolescents who have specific mental health disorders.)

127

## Following Instructions

When you are given an instruction, you should:

1. Look at the person who is talking.
2. Show that you understand by saying *"I under-stand,"* *"Okay,"* or *"I'll do it."* Sometimes, nodding your head will be enough.
3. Do what is asked in the best way you can.
4. Let the person know that you have finished.

### Possible reasons:

1. It is important to do what is asked because it shows your that you are able to cooperate and it saves time.
2. Following instructions will help you in school, in the home, and with adults and friends.

## Accepting Criticism

When others tell you how they think you can improve, they give you criticism. When you accept criticism, you should:

1. Look at the person. Don't make funny faces.
2. Remain calm and quiet while the person is talking.
3. Show that you understand. (Say *"Okay"* or *"I understand."*)
4. Try to correct the problem. If you are asked to do something different, do it. If you are asked to stop doing something, stop it. If you can't give a positive response, give one that is neutral. (Say *"Okay,"* *"I understand,"* or *"Thanks."*)

**Possible reasons:**

1. Being able to accept criticism shows maturity and prevents problems with people in authority.

2. If you can control yourself and listen to what others have to say about how you can improve, you'll have fewer problems.

3. The criticism may really help you improve the way you do something.

## Accepting "No" Answers

When someone gives you a "No" answer, you should:
1. Look at the person.
2. Say *"Okay."*
3. Calmly ask for a reason if you really don't understand.
4. If you disagree, bring it up later.

**Possible reasons:**

1. You will be told "No" many times in your life.

2. Getting angry and upset only leads to more problems.

3. If you are able to appropriately accept a "No" answer, people will view you as cooperative and mature.

## Staying Calm

It's hard for people to stay calm when they feel angry or upset. Many times, when you "blow up" you make poor choices that you later regret. If you feel that you are going to lose self-control, you should do one or more of the following:

1. Take a deep breath.
2. Relax your muscles.
3. Tell yourself to "be calm," or count to 10.
4. Share your feelings. After you are relaxed, tell someone you trust what is bothering you.
5. Leave or try to solve the situation that made you upset.

**Possible reasons:**

1. It is important to stay calm because things always seem to get worse when you lose your temper.
2. If you can stay calm, other people will depend on you more often.
3. People will see you as mature and able to handle even the worst situations.
4. Teachers and employers will respect you and view you as someone who can keep "cool."

## Disagreeing Appropriately

When you don't agree with another person's opinion or decision, you should:

1. Remain calm.
2. Look at the person.
3. Start by telling the person why you disagree with a positive or neutral statement. *("I know you are try-ing to be fair, but...")*

4. Explain why you disagree with the decision. Keep your voice tone controlled. Be brief and clear.

5. Listen as the other person explains his or her side of the story.

6. Calmly accept whatever decision is made.

7. Thank the person for listening, regardless of what happens.

**Possible reasons:**

1. Disagreeing in a calm manner increases the chances that the other person will listen.

2. You may have only one opportunity to get a decision changed; disagreeing appropriately gives you a better chance for success.

3. You have a right to express your opinions. But you lose that right if you become upset or aggressive.

4. If the other person feels that you are going to lose self-control, you might not be able to get your views across.

## Asking for Help

When you need help with something, you should:

1. Decide what the problem is.

2. Ask to speak to the person who is most likely to help you.

3. Look at the person, clearly describe what you need help with, and ask the person for help in a pleasant voice tone.

4. Thank the person for helping you.

**Possible reasons:**

1. It is important to ask for help from others because it often is the best way to solve problems you can't figure out.

2. Asking for help in a pleasant manner makes it more likely that someone will help you.

## Asking Permission

When you need to get permission from someone else, you should:

1. Look at the other person.

2. Be specific about what you are asking permission for.

3. Be sure to ask rather than demand. (Say *"May I please...?"*)

4. Give reasons if necessary.

5. Accept the decision.

**Possible reasons:**

1. It is important to ask permission whenever you want to do something or use something that belongs to another person. This shows your respect for others and their property and increases the chances that your request will be granted.

## Getting Along with Others

To be successful in dealing with people, you should:

1. Listen to what the other person has to say.

2. Say something positive if you agree with what the person said. If you don't agree, say something that won't result in an argument.

3. Use a calm voice tone.

4. Show interest in what the other person has to say. Try to understand his or her point of view.

**Possible reasons:**

1. It is important to get along with others because you will be working and dealing with other people all your life.

2. If you can get along with others, it is more likely that you will be successful in whatever you do.

3. Getting along with others shows sensitivity and respect.

4. If you can get along with others, it is more likely that they will behave the same way. In other words, treat others the way you want to be treated!

## Apologizing

When you have done something that hurts another person's feelings or results in negative consequences for another person, you should:

1. Look at the person.

2. Say what you are sorry about. (*"I'm sorry I said that..."* or *"I'm sorry, I didn't listen to what you said."*)

3. Make a follow-up statement if the person says something to you. (*"Is there any way I can make it up to you?"* or *"It won't happen again."*)

133

4. Thank the person for listening (even if the person did not accept your apology).

**Possible reasons:**

1. It is important to apologize because it shows that you are sensitive to the feelings of others.

2. It increases the chances that other people will be sensitive to your feelings in return.

3. Apologizing also shows that you are responsible enough to admit to making a mistake.

## Conversation Skills

When you are talking with someone, you should:

1. Look at the other person.

2. Answer any questions the person asks, and give complete answers.

3. Avoid negative statements.

4. Use appropriate words.

5. Start or add to the conversation by asking questions, talking about new or exciting events, or asking the other person what he or she thinks about something.

**Possible reasons:**

1. It is important to have good conversation skills because you can tell others what you think about something and find out how they feel.

2. Good conversation skills make guests feel more comfortable and make visits with you more enjoyable.

3. Conversation skills also help when you apply for a job or meet new people.

## Giving Compliments

When you want to say something nice about someone, you should:

1. Look at the other person.
2. Give the compliment. Tell him or her exactly what you liked.
3. Make a follow-up statement. If the person says, *"Thanks,"* you can say, *"You're welcome."*

**Possible reasons:**
1. Giving compliments shows that you notice the accomplishments of others.
2. It shows friendliness; people like being around someone who is pleasant and can say nice things.
3. It shows that you have confidence in your ability to talk to others.

## Accepting Compliments

Whenever someone says something nice to you, you should:

1. Look at the other person.
2. Listen to what the other person is saying.
3. Don't interrupt.
4. Say *"Thanks"* or something that shows you appreciate what was said.

**Possible reasons:**

1. Being able to accept compliments shows that you can politely receive another person's opinion about something that you have done.

2. It increases the chance that you will receive future compliments.

## Listening to Others

When others are speaking, you should:

1. Look at the person who is talking.

2. Sit or stand quietly.

3. Wait until the person is through talking. Don't interrupt.

4. Show that you understand by saying something like *"Thanks"* or *"I see."*

5. Ask the person to explain if you don't understand.

**Possible reasons:**

1. It is important to listen because it shows pleasantness and cooperation.

2. It increases the chances that people will listen to you.

3. It increases the chances that you will do the correct thing since you understand what you're supposed to do.

## Telling the Truth

To tell the truth, you should:

1. Look at the person.

2. If asked to supply information, say exactly what happened.

3. Answer any other questions. This can include what you did or did not do or what someone else did or did not do.

4. Don't leave out important facts.

5. Admit to mistakes or errors if you made them.

**Possible reasons:**

1. It is important to tell the truth because people are more likely to give you a second chance if they have been able to trust you in the past.

2. We all make mistakes, but lying or trying to cover up the truth will lead to more problems.

3. If you get a reputation as a liar, it will be hard for people to believe what you say.

4. When you tell the truth, you should feel confident that you have done the right thing.

## Introducing Yourself

When you introduce yourself to others, you should:

1. Stand up straight. If you were sitting down or doing something else, stop and greet the person.

2. Look at the other person.

3. Offer your hand and shake hands firmly. (Don't wait!)

4. As you are shaking hands, say your name clearly and loudly enough to be heard.

5. Make a friendly statement. *("Nice to meet you.")*

**Possible reasons:**

1. It is important to introduce yourself because it shows that you are able to meet new people confidently.

2. It makes others feel more comfortable and you make a good first impression.

3. Being able to introduce yourself will be helpful in job interviews and is a pleasant way to "break the ice."

# Social Skill Teaching Situations

Now, let's put social skill teaching in the context of some possible real-life events. The following examples give a situation and the social skill you'd probably choose to teach.

## Examples

You want your 9-year-old foster child to take out the garbage.

Skill to Teach: *Following Instructions*

You don't want your 12-year-old foster child to go to a concert that you believe is inappropriate for him or her.

Skill to Teach: *Accepting "No" for an Answer*

Your 6-year-old foster child eats some candy just before dinner.

Skill to Teach: *Asking Permission*

# Social Skills and Inappropriate Behavior

Learning skills will give foster children a positive way to get their needs met and to correct inappropriate behavior. You will be the child's primary teacher for these positive skills that can be used in place of inappropriate behaviors.

Let's look at some examples of possible skills that can be taught in response to a child's inappropriate behaviors.

## Examples

Your 13-year-old foster child argues, *"I didn't do it; you didn't see me,"* when you describe his inappropriate behavior.

Skills to Teach: *Accepting Criticism, Disagreeing Appropriately*

Your 7-year-old foster child flops down in a chair and pouts after you tell her she can't watch a movie because it's bedtime.

Skill to Teach: *Accepting "No" for an Answer*

Your 10-year-old foster child walks into the kitchen with her math book and says, *"Do this for me. I don't get it."*

Skill to Teach: *Asking for Help*

Your 14-year-old foster child pushes another child at school for not giving him the basketball during recess right away.

Skill to Teach: *Getting Along with Others*

# Choosing Social Skills

When deciding what skill to teach, ask yourself, *"What do I want the child to do instead?"* and *"What behavior(s) do I and others in society expect here?"* The following situations will help you recognize what skill(s) you might choose to teach.

## Examples

Your 6-year-old foster child refuses to put his coat and shoes on when it is time for school.
Teach the Skill: *Following Instructions*

Your 11-year-old foster child argues when you tell her she has lost some TV time for not doing her chore.
Teach the Skill: *Accepting Consequences*

Your 7-year-old foster child does not apologize for breaking another child's toy.
Teach the Skill: *Apologizing*

Your 14-year-old foster child screams and slams doors when he is angry.
Teach the Skill: *Staying Calm*

Your 15-year-old foster child makes up a story to explain why she was late getting home from school.
Teach the Skill: *Telling the Truth*

## Summary

This chapter has discussed how and why you should teach children social skills. By describing the specific components of a skill, foster children will learn to recognize when, where, how, and with whom to use these new behaviors. This will also give foster children the chance to learn that using these new skills will help them get their needs met appropriately. As foster children practice and use these new skills, they will be more successful in your home, in school, and in other environments. Ultimately, this will give them a better chance of successfully returning home or moving on to another living situation, and of becoming a well-adjusted, successful adult.

# CHAPTER 8

# The ABCs of Behavior

When working with foster children, it's sometimes easy to think about helping them change their behaviors only by responding after the behavior occurs. We have already talked about punishment versus teaching and discipline. But there is another opportunity when you can influence a child's behavior, and over time, change it. That is before the behavior happens. In the ABCs of behavior, what happens or exists before a behavior occurs is called the **antecedent.** ABC stands for:

| ABC | Example |
|---|---|
| **A = Antecedent** | You approach a stop sign. |
| **B = Behavior** | Instead of coming to a full stop, you roll through the intersection. |
| **C = Consequence** | A police officer sees this and gives you a ticket. |

We've already defined **behavior** as what a person does or says that can be seen, heard, or measured. A **consequence** is the outcome or result of an action. In this chapter, we'll first focus on **antecedents** and their role in changing a child's behavior, then move to a discussion of consequences.

## Antecedents

Understanding how antecedents can be identified and modified is another key to effective foster parenting. The best way to identify antecedents is to ask yourself the following questions about what is going on around a child before he or she does something:

**Who** is present when the behavior occurs?

**When** does the behavior occur?

**Where** does the behavior occur?

**What activity** is the foster child engaged in when the behavior occurs?

**What was said** to the foster child, and **how** was it said?

Using these questions as a guide, you can eventually learn to predict when certain behaviors might occur because the same events are occurring whenever a child uses that behavior. This gives you an advantage in heading off disruptive or negative behavior and enables you to make real progress in helping the kids in your care change their behavior for the better.

Here is a common scenario for any parent or Foster Parent who's ever taken a child shopping. After reading it, go through the questions that follow to identify the antecedents. Then we'll discuss how a Foster Parent could change or modify the antecedents in order to help prevent or stop the behavior from occurring in the future.

Julia, a foster mom, and her 8-year-old foster daughter, Samantha, are at the grocery store. After 30 minutes, they head down the candy aisle and Samantha asks for a candy bar. Julia says *"No."* Samantha begins to argue and shouts, *"I want a candy bar RIGHT NOW!"* When Julia tells her *"No"* again, Samantha's behavior gets worse, and she begins to cry and jump up and down. Then Samantha tells Julia that her "real mom" bought her candy whenever she wanted it, and, if Julia loved her, she would too. Other shoppers are watching the two now and Julia becomes frustrated. She wants to tell Samantha that if she were the girl's "real mom," she would be tempted to spank her when they left the store. Instead, Julia threatens to send Samantha to her room for the rest of the day when they get home.

When Julia and Samantha reach the checkout counter, both are clearly upset. Samantha grabs a candy bar from the display rack and demands that Julia buy it for her. Julia warns Samantha that she is getting tired of her behavior and tells her to put the candy back. Julia then takes the candy bar from Samantha. Samantha drops to the floor and screams. Now everyone is watching. Finally, Julia has had enough. She grabs the candy bar and gives it to Samantha. *"Now will you please be quiet and get up?"* Julia asks. Samantha takes the candy bar, gets up, and stops crying.

**Who** is present? *Julia, Samantha, and other people in the store*

**Where** are they? *In a grocery store*

**When** does the behavior occur? *Starts in the candy aisle and continues at the checkout counter*

**What** is the activity? *Grocery shopping*

Here are a few ways Julia could change the antecedents that led to Samantha's tantrum in the store:

- If Julia wanted to buy Samantha a snack, she could tell Samantha exactly what she must do to *earn* the snack. For example, Julia could tell Samantha that she has to wait until they get to the checkout counter before she can choose her treat, or that she must ask for a treat politely, without whining. If Julia does not want Samantha to have candy, Julia could let her earn something else by using appropriate behaviors while shopping. A reward might be playing dolls together later in the day or stopping at the park on the way home.
- Julia could let Samantha pick out a nutritional treat before they get to the candy aisle.
- Julia could avoid the aisle and checkout lane where there are candy displays.

- Julia could give Samantha lots of praise for good behavior (not whining or complaining, helping put groceries in the cart, pushing the cart), starting when they enter the store.

Observing and acting on antecedents is a skill that takes time and practice to do well, especially if you are used to responding to a behavior after it happens. But the benefits to both you and child are worth the effort. Changing antecedents can often help to head off inappropriate behaviors before they happen and bring about real progress with the children in your care.

## Consequences

Consequences are a part of everyone's life. For every action or behavior, there is a result or an outcome. Some consequences are natural. For example, if you go out in the rain without an umbrella, you get wet. Some consequences are what we call "applied." This means that someone intentionally gives or causes a consequence to happen after a behavior. For example, if you speed in your car, you may get a traffic ticket from a police officer. In the Girls and Boys Town model of care, applied consequences are one of the main ways we help teach skills to foster children.

> Consequences are powerful motivators for youngsters.

As a Foster Parent, you already understand how important a role consequences play in teaching and helping kids change their behaviors. Consequences help children learn that their choices determine what will happen to them. The results – or consequences – of their behavior can be either positive or negative. Once children understand the connection between how they behave and the results or consequences, they can begin to make better choices about how they think and act.

Consequences are powerful motivators for youngsters. As a Foster Parent (and a parent), you are very familiar with them! Taking a youth out for ice cream after she cleans her room, having a child go to time-out for throwing a tantrum, and letting a child have extra dessert for finishing his vegetables are all examples of consequences. But simply giving a child a positive or a negative consequence won't automatically bring about desired changes. Teaching, combined with a positive relationship and genuine caring, changes behaviors.

In this chapter, we'll take a closer look at what appropriate consequences are, how to choose the ones to use, and how they can be given while maintaining a positive Foster Parent-child relationship.

## Kinds of Consequences

There are two basic types of consequences – positive and negative. Let's define each one and look at some of the basic elements that make them effective.

**Positive consequences** are things that people like and are willing to work for. Behavior that is followed by a positive consequence is more likely to occur again (or will occur more frequently). Rewards like candy, verbal encouragement, and a hug are forms of positive consequences.

**Negative consequences** are things people don't like or want to avoid. Basically, negative consequences teach kids to change their actions so that they won't receive more negative consequences. Behavior that is followed by a negative consequence is less likely to occur again (or will not occur as frequently). Removing a privilege (phone, TV, video game) or adding a chore or task (cleaning the kitchen, taking out the trash) are examples of negative consequences.

> Changing antecedents can often help to head off inappropriate behaviors before they happen.

As we said earlier, simply giving consequences doesn't necessarily help children learn new behaviors or change old ones. Consequences must have certain qualities if they are to be effective. These qualities include:

## Importance

A consequence has to mean something to your foster child. One way to find out what is important to your foster children is to watch what they do during their free time. For example, if a child likes to watch TV, invite friends over to your house, and ride his bicycle, then these activities are important to your foster child. These everyday and special activities can be used as consequences. Having a child earn something that he or she isn't interested in or taking something away that he or she doesn't care about will likely have little effect on behavior.

## Immediacy

This means giving a consequence right after a behavior occurs. If you can't deliver the consequence right away, do it as soon as possible. Delaying a consequence reduces its impact and weakens the connection between the behavior and the consequence. For example, rewarding your foster child by letting him stay up late to watch a show two weeks after he helped you with yard work, or taking playtime away from your 5-year-old foster daughter for something she did three days ago will only confuse the children. Neither child will link the consequence to earlier behavior, and the 5-year-old will probably think you are being tremendously unfair. In some situations, a consequence might involve an event that will occur in the future (a weekend trip to the park). In this case, you should tell your foster child what the consequence is right after the behavior occurs.

> **Try to deliver the smallest consequence you think will be effective.**

## Frequency

This refers to the number of times a consequence is given. If you give the same consequence too often or too seldom, it will lose its effectiveness. Changes in a foster child's behavior will help you determine whether you are using a consequence the right amount of time. For example, if you were to give your foster child a piece of candy (assuming he loved it) each time he helped around the house, and he soon started showing less interest in helping you, it might indicate that candy has lost its appeal as a consequence because you've given it too often.

Ideally, when you are teaching a child a new behavior, you should deliver a positive consequence for the appropriate behavior *each* and *every time* it occurs, *immediately* after it occurs. Once the foster child has learned the new skill and can use it without being reminded, you can begin to deliver the positive consequence *intermittently* (every other time the child uses the behavior or occasionally). This will help ensure that the behavior continues to happen and allows you to move your attention to teaching new skills.

## Size

This means that the size of the consequence should fit the behavior; the consequence shouldn't be too big or too small. Typically, Foster Parents should try to deliver the smallest consequence they think will be effective. This goes for both positive and negative consequences. If you think that allowing your foster child to have a friend stay over on a weekend night will be incentive enough for her to keep her room clean during the week, use it as the positive consequence. On the other hand, grounding a foster child for a month for not cleaning her room would be too big of a negative consequence. A less severe consequence (not allowing her to have her friend stay over) would probably get the job done. The problem with giving positive consequences that are too "big" is that they may "spoil" the foster child, who now gets too much for doing too little. On the other hand, giving large negative consequences for relatively minor misbehavior may make the foster child feel like he or she is always being punished. The child may give up trying to change because the consequences are too great if she makes a mistake.

## Contingency

Contingency means that a privilege your foster child likes is available only after the child finishes an activity he or she is asked to do. This is commonly called "Grandma's rule" because grandmothers used it long before it ever showed up in a book. Some examples are:

- *"You may watch TV after you have finished your homework."*
- *"You may go outside after you make your bed and put your dirty clothes in the laundry basket."*
- *"When you have finished the dishes, you may call your friend."*

"Grandma's rule," or tying a privilege to completion of a specified task, can be used with foster children of all ages.

## Thinking Ahead

It's wise to set up both positive and negative consequences in advance. For example, when your foster daughter does not do her chores, both of you should know what the negative consequences could be. If your foster son does what is expected, he should know what positive consequences to expect. As you get to know your foster child better, you will learn what positive and negative consequences are most effective. Just like with your own children, these change over time as your foster child changes and grows.

Your foster children should be aware of any planned consequences. Don't hesitate to post established consequences, both positive and negative, on your refrigerator door or in your foster children's rooms. Consequences shouldn't be surprises. In fairness to your foster children, they should be aware of what they will earn for behaving well and what they will lose for misbehavior. In this way, they are in control because they know that their behavior determines what consequences they earn. This helps your foster child learn how choices affect what happens to him or her.

> **Consequences shouldn't be surprises.**

## Giving Consequences

Later chapters will outline steps for effectively delivering consequences to your foster child. For now, here are a few basic components that will help you understand how to deliver consequences so they have a positive effect on a child's behavior.

When delivering a consequence, remember to do the following:

**Be clear.**

Make sure your foster child knows what the consequence is and what he or she did to earn it.

**Be consistent.**

Don't deliver a big consequence for a behavior one time and then ignore the same behavior the next time. This goes for both positive and negative behaviors. Also, decide when a behavior is inappropriate enough to merit a consequence. For most Foster Parents, there is a fine line between acceptable and unacceptable behavior. This line is a Foster Parent's "tolerance level." A Foster Parent with a low tolerance level gives consequences as soon as the misbehavior begins and before it becomes severe. A Foster Parent with a high tolerance level waits until after a behavior occurs repeatedly or get worse before giving a consequence. It's best to have a low, but fair, tolerance level with a foster child. Each person must decide when "enough is enough."

Spouses may generally agree on where to draw the line regarding misbehavior, but it is very difficult, if not impossible, to always agree on everything. The important thing is to talk with your spouse about when to start delivering consequences for appropriate behavior and misbehavior, and then *consistently follow through with your teaching and consequences.* Your foster children will be less confused and they will view you as being fair. In the long run, it is less likely that children will view one Foster Parent as the "good guy" and the other as the "bad guy." If you and your spouse cannot agree, or you regularly differ on consequences, you should sit down together, discuss the situation, and come to agreement on these issues.

**Be brief.**

This is especially true with younger children who may have shorter attention spans. Clear messages usually get lost when you lecture.

**Follow through.**

If you set up an arrangement for your foster child to earn a positive consequence, be sure he or she gets the reward after the task is completed. Likewise, if you give a negative consequence, don't let your foster child talk you out of it (unless you decide that the consequence you gave was unreasonable or given out of anger).

**Be as pleasant as possible.**

This is easier to do when you give positive consequences, but it's also important to be pleasant when you deliver negative consequences. Yelling and screaming are turn-offs to kids and are not effective. They can't hear your words; they only hear (and see) your anger. Girls and Boys Town's research shows that foster children are more likely to respond positively and learn more from adults who are calm and reasonable, even when the adults are delivering negative consequences. Being pleasant also is important to maintaining a healthy, caring relationship with your foster child. Whether you are giving a positive or negative consequence, your mannerisms and behavior should show that you care about the child.

# When Consequences Don't Work

Occasionally, Foster Parents feel that no matter what they try, the consequences they are using aren't working with their foster child. There could be several reasons for this.

First, we can all get frustrated and begin to focus on the negative behaviors and give too many negative consequences, while neglecting positive behaviors and positive consequences. As a result, foster children feel like they can never do anything right and they stop responding to most negative consequences. And foster children start to look elsewhere for positive consequences because it's just too unpleasant for them to be around their Foster Parents.

A second reason is that Foster Parents don't always give consequences enough time to work. They might expect a consequence to change a behavior the first time it is used. This typically isn't the case. Change takes time. Foster children didn't learn to behave the way they do, good or bad, overnight. Therefore, Foster Parents need to be patient, look for small improvements, and give the consequences time to work.

In addition, Foster Parents may not make the connection between a child's behavior and the consequence clear to him or her. So, the child does not change the behavior because he or she doesn't understand that a certain behavior results in a consequence.

Finally, some Foster Parents mistake privileges for rights. Of course, most foster children will try to convince their Foster Parents that everything is a right. But if Foster Parents treat privileges as rights, they limit what they can use for consequences. The rights of foster children include the right to nourishment, communication with others, clothing, and so on. (See Chapter 4.) Watching TV, going out with friends, and using family possessions all are privileges that can and should be monitored by the Foster Parents and used by the foster child with approval.

## Warnings and Threats

Many Foster Parents have fallen prey to giving too many warnings: *"For the third time, I'll take your game away if you don't stop that."* While a single warning may be effective, repeated warnings that are not followed by consequences usually do not work and become a source of frustration for Foster Parents. If you have to come back time after time to deal with the same behavior, you may be talking too much and not following through with consequences. If you tell your foster child that you will take away a game for a certain misbehavior, and the misbehavior occurs, then take the game away for a period of time. This helps the child understand that there are rules in your family and that you expect everyone to follow them. Otherwise, rules become confusing and turn obedience into a guessing game for your child: *"Can I get away with it this time? My foster mom has warned me three times, and nothing's happened yet."*

One last point about consequences: Sometimes, out of frustration, Foster Parents make the mistake of threatening a child's placement in an attempt to "shock" the foster child or emphasize the seriousness of the situation.

Although this may be done with good intentions, it almost always has a negative effect. Threatening to remove a child from your home will damage your relationship, hurt the child, and, ultimately, make your consequences less effective. Remember that many foster children already wonder if you really want them; they are ready to push people away so that they aren't "abandoned" or rejected once again. Threatening to throw them out makes this fear more real.

## Summary

Focusing on antecedents and giving consequences through teaching are important ingredients to helping foster children change behavior. When you follow the suggestions discussed in this chapter your teaching and consequences will become more effective.

# CHAPTER 9

# Rewarding Good Behavior

Positive consequences are referred to as **rewards.** Generally, these are things that people like or enjoy and are willing to work for. When Foster Parents use positive consequences to reward positive behavior, that behavior is likely to occur again or occur more often. Over time, this helps the child to either learn a new skill or behavior or get better at one they already use.

For many adults, "catching kids being good" is unnatural and awkward; oftentimes, they expect kids to automatically know how to do the right thing and make correct choices. The reality is that kids make mistakes. They don't do everything adults would like them to do and more often than not, these mistakes are glaring and easy to spot – much easier than the times when kids do the right thing or make good choices.

Unfortunately, it's human nature to focus on the negative. Read today's newspaper or watch the evening news. Most stories are about negative events, not positive ones.

When it comes to teaching, Foster Parents can fall into the same trap: They expect and ignore appropriate behavior, while focusing most of their attention and teaching on inappropriate behavior. But children also do many good things, and it's up to Foster Parents to recognize and reward those behaviors. That's where positive consequences can be a Foster Parent's best friend.

As we said earlier, when children earn only negative consequences, they become discouraged and may feel that they can't do anything right. In these situations, foster children may want to avoid their Foster Parents. The alternative also is true. When foster children earn positive consequences, they feel more successful and want to spend more time with their Foster Parents. This provides even more opportunities for Foster Parents to look for and reinforce positive behavior. In addition, Foster Parents who equitably balance out positive and negative consequences are viewed by foster children as being more fair, reasonable, pleasant, and effective. All this makes it more likely that children will listen and respond favorably to teaching.

## Positive Consequences That Work

One of the most important factors to remember about positive consequences is that something that is a reward for one child may not be a reward for another child. The old saying, "Different strokes for different folks," applies here. Some children might like tangible rewards like a special outing or an extra snack. Others might prefer public praise, pats on the back, or spending time with you playing a board game. The key is to discover what your foster child likes and to use those things as positive consequences in your teaching.

How can you find out what foster children like? It's pretty simple: Watch facial expressions, listen to voice tones, what they ask for, music they listen to, hobbies, and other interests. Plus, why not simply ask them? You may be surprised by what you learn. Remember, for positive consequences to be effective, they must be meaningful to children.

> Children do many good things, and it's up to Foster Parents to recognize and reward those behaviors.

The following categories are guides that can help you to find the positive consequences that will work with your foster child. Note: You'll notice that some of the suggested rewards cost money, and some do not. It would be impracticable, if not impossible, to run out and buy something every time your foster child behaves well. Even if you could, it wouldn't be healthy for the foster child. So remember that rewards don't have to be something you buy. (On page 163 is a list of "freebies" that make great rewards.)

## Categories of Positive Consequences

**Activities** – What everyday activities does your foster child like (video games, baseball, watching sitcoms, baking cookies, reading)?

161

**Possessions** – What material articles does your foster child like (sweatshirts, baseball cards, money, dolls, compact discs)?

**Special Activities** – What special activities does your foster child like (going to a ball game, visiting a zoo, going to a movie, having a friend stay overnight)?

**Special Snacks** – What are your foster child's favorite foods and beverages (popcorn, cupcakes, pizza, cola, candy, fruit juice)? Remember: Do *not* use meals as a negative consequence. As stated in Chapter 4, "Creating a Safe Environment," foster children have the right to proper nutrition. Only special snacks and/or "extras" should be used as a consequence.

**People** – With whom does your foster child like to spend time (appropriate friends, foster parents, other foster children, or others)? Remember: A foster child's opportunity to visit with his or her family is not a reward; it is a right unless the court or the foster child's caseworker or legal guardian has determined that seeing the family would be harmful to the child.

**Attention** – What specific kinds of verbal and physical attention from you and others does your foster child like (hugs, smiles, compliments, high fives, thumbs up, praise)?

**Other Rewards** – Is there anything else that your foster child likes, is interested in, or would like to spend time doing? Is there a favorite chore, or something that he or she has wanted to do but hasn't yet done?

## Positive Consequences That Cost No Money

Stay up late

Stay out late (supervised)

Have a friend over

Pick the TV program

Extra TV (or video game) time

One less chore

Pick a movie (with approval)

Foster Parent reads a story at night

Stay up late reading

Permission for a special event

Dinner in the family room

Extra time on the computer

Bike ride or fishing trip

Indoor picnic

Extra phone time

Messy room for a day

Leave the radio on at night

Go over to a friend's house

Sit at the head of the table

Pick an outing

Shorter study period

Decide where to go for dinner

Trip to library, zoo, pet store, park

Play game with Foster Parent

Special snacks

Sleep late

Pick the breakfast cereal

Plan the menu

Remove a chore

# Shaping

Sometimes, using positive consequences may not be enough to get a foster child to start changing a behavior. This is particularly true if you are trying to teach a new set of skills that a foster child is having difficulty learning. In these situations, you can use shaping. Simply put, **shaping** means praising or reinforcing a foster child's *attempts* to use the new skill you are teaching.

For example, if your foster child is not used to making his bed and cleaning his room, you would enthusiastically praise and reward him for pulling his covers up on the bed and putting his toys away in the corner of the room. This may be less than you ultimately want, but the child is making an effort to follow your instructions and clean his room. Next time, you may ask the foster child to put his dirty clothes in the hamper, in addition to making the bed and picking up his toys. Eventually, the foster child will be able to clean his room on his own. You will have shaped the skill (making a bed and cleaning a room) one step at a time through specific teaching, praise, and positive consequences for each attempt along the way. This helps the child feel that he can accomplish what is expected of him.

Many foster children with low self-confidence give up before they really try. Shaping helps the foster child "bite off a little at a time" until his or her confidence has improved.

## Bribes

The idea of using positive consequences (or rewards) to change behaviors is viewed with skepticism by some Foster Parents. To them, it seems that foster children are being bribed or paid off for doing what they're expected to do. However, rewards are a natural part of daily life. They can include anything from the obvious, like ice cream for a good report card, to more subtle rewards, like a smile or a wink. These are delivered for acceptable behavior, behavior that Foster Parents would like to see repeated.

Bribery occurs when positive consequences are given for *inappropriate* behavior. Giving a child a candy bar at the grocery store checkout lane to make her stop crying is a bribe. At the time, it may seem neces-

> **Rewards are a natural part of daily life.**

sary for your sanity, and you may feel like doing anything to stop your foster daughter's negative behavior. *("Okay, you can have the candy. Just stop crying!")* In the end, however, the child is rewarded for engaging in inappropriate behavior. The reward stopped the foster child's crying at that moment, but guess what happens the next time she is in the checkout lane with you? Right! The child cries and demands a candy bar. (Remember that our children are constantly using consequences with us just as we are using consequences with them.) The child has learned that crying (an inappropriate behavior) will get her a candy bar; she has been bribed and she's learned that crying will get another bribe the next time she wants something.

Foster children should not earn rewards for inappropriate behaviors: Those are bribes. Instead, foster children should earn rewards only for using positive behaviors.

Using this example, here's how the candy bar could be used as a positive consequence: You may tell your foster child that if she stays next to the cart, does not touch items on the shelf, and does not complain, she can pick out a candy bar when you've finished shopping. The difference here is that you are setting your expectations and rewarding (and reinforcing) positive behaviors.

## Summary

Consistently and correctly using positive consequences to reward positive behaviors makes it more likely that you will see the children in your care use those positive behaviors. Find out what your foster child likes and use these things as positive consequences in your teaching. Remember, the most powerful rewards for foster children can be praise and positive attention from you. Continue to focus on the positive things your foster children do. Positive consequences work!

# CHAPTER 10

# Giving Negative Consequences

*"I hate you!"*

*"I don't have to do anything I don't want to!"*

*"I was only an hour late. What's the big deal?"*

*"Why do I have to clean my room? I just cleaned it last week."*

Okay, so children won't earn positive consequences all of the time. They are going to say and do things that you don't like. When kids do, they should receive negative consequences as part of your teaching. If the consequences are given in a firm, fair, and consistent manner, they will be effective and so will your teaching.

As a Foster Parent, one of your first goals should be to find out what negative consequences work best with your foster child. Just as with positive consequences, different negative consequences are effective with some foster children and not with others. The key to determining the effectiveness of a consequence is the result: Did the inappropriate behavior stop or occur less often when a particular consequence was used? If the misbehavior stops or occurs less, then the consequence is working. If the misbehavior continues, then the consequence isn't effective and a new one should be found and used.

In this chapter, we will concentrate on two forms of negative consequences: taking away a privilege and adding chores related to the misbehavior. These work best with children six years of age and older. Time-out, which will be discussed in the next chapter, works best with children younger than six.

## Removing a Privilege

When a problem behavior occurs, one type of negative consequence is the removal of a privilege. Some situations are tailor-made for this. For example, if your foster daughter comes home an hour late, you may remove part of her privilege of going out at night (coming home an hour earlier the next time she goes out). If this problem continues, she may lose the entire privilege of going out for a period of time. Similarly, if two young children are arguing about which TV show to watch, you can shut off the TV until you teach them how to settle their differences, or they can lose TV privileges for that evening.

> **If negative consequences are given in a firm, fair, and consistent manner, they will be effective.**

Using the method that was presented in Chapter 5, "Setting Expectations and Sending Clear Messages," you should combine clear messages with negative consequences. For example, you could tell your foster daughter, *"Sarah, since you came home one hour later than we agreed, you won't be able to go out tomorrow night."* In the example of the two young children arguing over the TV, you could say, *"Vinnie and Ray, you're arguing about which show to watch. Please shut the TV off so we can calmly discuss how to solve this."*

Always keep in mind the qualities that make consequences effective. During the first few weeks that your foster child is living with you, you may not be sure which negative consequences will be effective. By talking with the foster child about his or her interests and talking with people who have cared for the child before, you will probably get some good ideas. As you get to know your foster child better, you will figure out what works and what doesn't work.

In deciding what consequence to use, you should ask yourself these questions: (We'll use the situation with Sarah coming home late as an example.)

**Is the consequence...**

- **Important?** Does Sarah really like to go out?
- **Immediate?** Can the consequence be given right away?
- **Being used too frequently?** Has Sarah lost the privilege of going out so often that she doesn't

really care anymore? Or does she enjoy watching TV so much that she doesn't mind staying home?

- **The right amount?** Will losing one night out with her friends be enough (or too much) of a consequence?

- **Contingent?** Can I use Grandma's Rule, making the privilege I'm taking away available only after Sarah finishes a specified task? *("If you come home from school on time for two days in a row, **then** you can earn the privilege of going out on Friday night.")*

## Adding Chores

Adding chores is an effective negative consequence for teaching kids to take responsibility for their behavior. Doing an extra chore takes time and effort, and if this takes away from the time children would spend doing something that's fun, they will try to avoid the consequence by changing their behavior.

When possible, the consequence should relate directly to the problem behavior. In fact, this type of consequence is designed to have kids "make up" for their misbehavior. (There may be times when you'll be unable to tie the consequence to the problem behavior. In these situations, you can simply add a chore.) So, instead of removing a privilege, you're having your foster child do something constructive in order to get your message across.

The process of adding a chore is simple. For example, if your foster son constantly leaves his clothes on the floor, he must pick them up before he gets to do what he wants to do (Grandma's Rule). Or, he must gather the dirty clothes from every family member and put them in the hamper.

Here are some other examples of how to add a chore as a consequence:

**Behavior:** Your foster son throws his clean clothes in the corner of his closet.

**Consequence:** He must fold those clothes as well as help you fold the next load of laundry.

**Behavior:** Your foster daughter doesn't take her lunch bag to school, so you have to take it to her.

**Consequence:** The next day, she must get up 15 minutes earlier than normal so she has enough time to prepare her lunch.

**Behavior:** Your son and foster child are fighting about who emptied the dishwasher the last time.

**Consequence:** To help them learn how to get along, you have them empty the dishwasher together the next two nights.

It is important to use caution when adding a chore as a consequence for negative behavior. While most chores are corrective and very acceptable, it is possible to overdo it. Limiting the number of extra chores a child earns and ensuring that they relate to the negative behavior are two ways to avoid misusing this type of consequence. Meaningless work (digging a hole and then filling it back up, moving blocks back and forth between two places) should *never* be used as a consequence.

## Giving Negative Consequences

The effectiveness of your consequences depends, in part, on how you give them. An angry response is not going to work; it will likely result in more problems. Our experience shows that children respond better and learn more from adults who are pleasant and positive, even when they are giving negative consequences.

As mentioned earlier, Girls and Boys Town has developed a method called *Corrective Teaching*. This teaching method combines clear messages with consequences and practice to help you respond to problem behaviors. *Corrective Teaching* also provides you with a formula for giving consequences as part of your response to routine negative behaviors. For now, it's enough to only mention this teaching method; it is described in detail in Chapter 15. But we do want you to know that negative consequences are given as part of a focused, organized teaching process.

## Is the Consequence Truly Negative?

Sometimes, Foster Parents make the mistake of assuming that a consequence is negative simply because it involves taking away a privilege or adding a chore. The only way to determine if the consequence is working is to look at the effect it has on the behavior you want a child to change. If you consistently give a *negative consequence* during teaching, you should see an inappropriate behavior *occur less often or stop.* (Conversely, consistently giving a *positive consequence* should lead a child to *continue or use a certain behavior more often.*) When a negative consequence is not having the desired effect, it may be because it's not really a negative consequence.

Here's a real-life example: A foster mother told us that her 6-year-old foster son continually fidgeted and talked in church. She told him that he couldn't come with her next time if he continued causing problems in church. Sure enough, the boy fidgeted like crazy and talked more than ever. Why? He didn't want to be in church to begin with! His foster mother's "negative consequence" actually encouraged more problem behaviors. The behavior she wanted to stop increased. So, in reality, she had unwittingly delivered a positive consequence. In this situation, the foster mother could use one of the following consequences to stop the boy's misbehaviors:

- **Remove a privilege** – The boy can't play with his friend after church if he fidgets during the service.

- **Add work** – The boy has to stay after the service is over and put away all the hymnals and other books that were left in the pews.

Remember: The person who is receiving the consequence determines whether it is positive or negative, while the person giving the consequence can determine whether the consequence is positive or negative only by observing how it affects the behavior.

## The Snowball Effect

One problem with negative consequences is that Foster Parents can lose sight of when to stop. If one consequence doesn't work, they often try another that is larger and harsher. This can create an upward spiral of consequences that result, for example, in the foster child being grounded for the next five months or receiving some other unreasonable consequence that Foster Parents can't follow through on. This is called the "snowball effect." This can be especially harmful when you are working with angry and aggressive kids. When children are already upset, using harsher consequences only makes matters worse. Over time, kids learn what your "hot buttons" are and they won't hesitate to push these buttons when they are upset. When Foster Parents lose their patience and become frustrated and angry, the consequences begin to pile up and get larger and larger, like a snowball rolling down a hill.

Consider this situation: Amy didn't clean her room, so her foster dad took away her telephone privileges for a weekend. Her room was still messy the next day. So foster dad took away a week of TV privileges. The room didn't get any cleaner the next day, so he added another month without phone privileges, another week without TV, and told her that she couldn't come out of her room until it was spotless.

Whew! This wasn't just the snowball effect; it was an avalanche! In three days, this girl lost just about all communication with the outside world! This is a good example of how Foster Parents can sometimes get carried away with ineffective negative consequences and, in the process, violate a foster child's rights. So, instead of firing off one negative consequence after another, take a step back and look at the effect the consequence is having on the behavior. Change the consequence if necessary, but don't continue to pile on consequence after consequence. *More is not necessarily better.*

Since the consequences given by the foster dad in the previous example were unreasonable, a better plan would be for him to help Amy clean her room, and in return, have her help him clean the garage.

If these two parts of the plan are completed, Amy could earn her privileges back. To help Amy keep her room clean on a consistent basis, the foster dad could use Grandma's Rule: Each day that Amy cleans her room, she gets to use the phone

> When children are already upset, using harsher consequences only makes matters worse.

and watch her favorite TV show. This is a practical solution that is likely to work. Amy's room may not be spotless, but it will probably be clean more often than it is dirty. And, the foster dad knows exactly what consequence to use, depending on whether the room is clean or dirty. He has learned how to avoid the snowball effect and still deliver a negative consequence that works.

Foster Parents must be willing to look at their own behavior when they are delivering negative consequences. They need to determine if they are delivering too many negative consequences or if the consequences are too extreme. If that is happening, Foster Parents should change the consequences they are using.

## Summary

Finding effective negative consequences is a challenge for Foster Parents, but it is not impossible. If your foster children misbehave, you can remove all or part of a privilege or add a chore. Be logical, fair, consistent, and don't overdo it. Do these things and you'll be on the road to using effective consequences.

# CHAPTER 11

# Using Time-In and Time-Out

One consequence that works well with younger children (six years old or younger) is **time-out.** This involves having a child sit in one place for a certain amount of time, away from all the enjoyable things in his or her life. Time-out works with most young kids because they eventually begin to realize that using appropriate behaviors helps them to stay out of time-out, allowing them to do things they like to do.

**Time-in,** the opposite of time-out, is an important concept that helps make time-out effective. So, before we explain how time-out works, let's discuss time-in.

## What Is Time-In?

In order to understand what time-out is and how it works, it's important to first know what time-in means. Time-in is the time a young child spends doing enjoyable, fun things – playing with you, coloring, drawing, reading, watching television, or anything else he or she likes to do.

Time-in is the "good stuff" in a child's life. Much of that enjoyment can come from being around you, especially when you make a point of praising the child for good behavior and develop a close, personal bond with him or her. Because time-in is so important to a child, taking it away for short periods can be a powerful consequence. Being taken away from time-in is called time-out.

## What Is Time-Out?

Time-out is a way of disciplining your foster child for misbehavior without raising your hand or your voice. Time-out involves removing your foster child from enjoyable activities, for a small amount of time, immediately after misbehavior. Time-out for children is similar to penalties used for hockey players. When a hockey player has misbehaved on the ice, he is required to go into the penalty area for a specific amount of time. The referee does not scream at, threaten, or hit the player. He merely blows the whistle and points to the penalty area. During the penalty time, the player is not allowed to play, only watch. Time-out bothers hockey players because they would rather play hockey than watch. With foster children, time-out can be effective because they would rather be doing something fun than quietly sitting alone.

## When to Use Time-Out

In general, time-out is used for aggressive behavior and for repeatedly not following instructions. It's important that you do not use time-out for every problem behavior. For minor behaviors, the child should earn a consequence, such as loss of a privilege. For more serious behaviors, you may use time-out.

You may use time-out as a consequence in your teaching to negative behaviors. Immediately following a problem behavior, tell your foster child what he or she did and send the child to time-out. For example, you might say, *"Hitting is not okay. Go to time-out."* Say this calmly and only once. Do not reason with or give long explanations to your foster child. Remember: You will teach to the behavior in a little while, but first you want to give your foster child a chance to calm down. In rare instances, your foster child may refuse to go to time-out, or may be too upset to do so (lying on the floor kicking and screaming). Wait for the child to calm down and follow through with the time-out.

> **Do not use time-out for every problem behavior.**

## Location of Time-Out

If possible, it's best to use the same place every time. It might be a chair in the kitchen, a step, or the couch. Make sure the area is well lit and free from any dangerous objects. Also, make sure your foster child cannot watch TV or play with toys during time-out. The main purpose of time-out is for your foster child to be alone and quiet with no outside reinforcement.

## Length of Time-Out

The upper limit should be one quiet minute for every year of your foster child's age. The amount of time your foster child spends in time-out will depend not only on the child's age, but also on his or her developmental level. Frequently, children in foster care are not at the same developmental level as other children their age. With this in mind, it may not be appropriate for a 5-year-old child to be in time-out for a full five minutes. This may be too long for him or her. Initially, the child may only be in time-out for a few minutes, with the goal of working up to the full five minutes.

Keep in mind that children usually do not like time-out, and they can express their opinions very strongly. So, although your goal may be to get a child to sit quietly for three minutes, it may take some time to achieve this goal. This is especially true in the beginning when children don't know the rules and still can't believe you are doing this to them. For some reason, the calmer you remain, the more upset they are likely to become.

> **A child must remain seated and quiet to get out of time-out.**

This is all part of the process. Discipline works best when you administer it calmly.

So, do not begin the time-out until your foster child is calm and quiet. If your foster son is crying, throwing a tantrum, swearing, or doing any of the other such behaviors kids do when they're upset, it doesn't count toward the required time. If you start the time-out when he is quiet but he starts to cry or throws a tantrum, wait until he is quiet again, then start the time over again. Do not let him out of time-out until he has calmed down. The child must remain seated and quiet to get out of time-out.

## What Counts as Quiet Time

Generally, quiet time occurs when your foster child is not angry or loud. You must decide when your foster child is calm and quiet. Some children get perfectly still and quiet while in time-out. Other children find it hard to sit still and not talk. Fidgeting and "happy talk" should usually count as calm and quiet. If, for example, your foster daughter sings or talks softly to herself, that counts as quiet time. If she is arguing or talking back, that does not count as quiet time.

## Dealing with Time-Out Misbehavior

If your foster child leaves the time-out area before time is up, calmly tell the child to go back to the time-out chair. If he doesn't respond, let him know what the consequence will be. For example, he may lose one or all of his privileges until he completes his time-out. Provide him with a short reason why it's important to finish his time-out: *"The sooner you finish time-out, the sooner you'll be able to do what you want to do."*

If your foster child misbehaves during time-out, say nothing. Ignore everything that is not dangerous to the child, to you, or to the furniture. Most negative behavior during time-out is an attempt to get you to react and say something. So expect the unexpected. Your foster child may whine, cry, complain, throw things, or make a big mess. He or she may make many unkind comments about you, your spouse, or your children. These types of comments are frustrating and may be hard to ignore. But remember: He or she is saying them to get a reaction out of you. Remaining calm and not responding is the best way to handle it. Don't worry. Your foster child will like you again after the time is up.

## When Time-Out Is Over

When the time-out period is over, ask your foster child, *"Are you ready to get up?"* Your foster child must answer *"Yes"* in some way (or nod yes) before he or she may get up. Go back and finish your teaching. Tell the child what you want him or her to do, and practice.

Once the time-out is over, be sure to look for and praise good behavior. Now is the time to reward your foster children for the kinds of behaviors you want them to use. So "catch 'em being good!"

## Explain Time-Out Rules

Explain the rules of time-out to your foster child before you use it. At a time when your foster child is not misbehaving, explain what time-out is, which problem behaviors time-out will be used for, and how long time-out will last. Practice time-outs with your foster child before using the procedure. While practicing, remind him or her that you are "pretending" this time. The child probably still will have difficulty when you do your first real time-outs, but follow through just the way you told your child you would.

---

## Time-Out Steps

1. Choose a time-out area.

2. Explain time-out.

3. Use time-out every time the problem behavior occurs.

4. Be specific and brief when you explain why your foster child must go to time-out.

5. Do not talk to or look at your foster child during time-out.

6. If your foster child gets up from time-out before the time is up, do some teaching about why he or she should stay in time-out, and provide reasons.

7. Your foster child must be calm and quiet to get up from time-out.

8. Your child must politely answer "Yes" when you ask, "Are you ready to get up?"

9. If you wanted your foster child to follow an instruction, give him or her another chance after time-out is over.

10. Catch your foster child being good.

---

## Summary

Remember: Time-out is most effective with younger kids (six years old or younger) and shouldn't be used with older children or adolescents. For these kids, it's usually more effective to deliver a consequence that removes something they like (loss of phone, TV, or computer privileges) or adds something they don't like (extra chore).

# CHAPTER 12

# Preventing Problems Before They Occur

Benjamin Franklin once said, "An ounce of prevention is worth a pound of cure." He was right; society's reliance on preventive measures is proof of that. We have fire drills; we get our cars tuned up; we go to the doctor for a physical exam. We take all of these precautionary measures to prevent problems from happening. While practicing a fire drill may not keep a fire from starting, it could prevent a catastrophe such as the loss of life in a fire. Prevention is both necessary and important.

## An Ounce of Prevention

Girls and Boys Town has taken Ben's wisdom, applied it, and developed a teaching method called *Proactive Teaching.* This is our "ounce of prevention." *Proactive Teaching* means teaching skills to foster children *before* they need to use the skills. Then, when foster children find themselves in situations where they should use a certain skill, they're better prepared to do so. This helps them head off and avoid problems that might have occurred in similar situations in the past. When kids know what is expected of them and have the opportunity to prepare for a situation, they are much more likely to be successful.

## Why Teach Proactively?

You've probably used what we call *Proactive Teaching* many times before – teaching your own children how to safely cross the street, what number they should dial in case of an emergency, what clothes they should wear when it's cold, and so on.

It's a simple concept, but many people don't use *Proactive Teaching* as often or in as many situations as they could. Many of the children in foster care have not had adults teach them the skills they will need to be successful within their family, at school, and in other social settings. You should not assume that children who come to your home know what you expect. *Proactive Teaching* and setting expectations go hand in hand. For example, in a previous placement, it may have been perfectly fine for a child to come home late from school without calling. In your foster home, your expectations may be for your foster child to come home on time or call if he or she is going to be late. These expectations need to be clearly communicated to your foster child. This is why teaching kids specific skills before they need to use them is so important. When you take the time to teach children skills, like *Following Instructions* or *Accepting 'No' Answers,* they will know what you expect and, in turn, will be better able to meet your expectations.

As discussed in Chapter 7, "Introduction to Teaching Social Skills," explaining the specific steps of various skills will help children learn those skills more quickly. For example, a common skill that most children need to learn or improve on when they come to your home is *Following Instructions.* While it may seem like common sense to you, many children do not know **You should not assume that children who come to your home know what you expect.** what you want them to do when you ask them to pick up their room. A child may assume that he can do it tomorrow or that he can throw all of his dirty clothes in the closet. Describing the steps to a skill ahead of time helps your foster child understand exactly what is expected.

## When to Use Proactive Teaching

There are two specific times when you should use *Proactive Teaching:*

1. When your foster child is learning something new.
2. When your foster child has had difficulty in a past situation and is going to face the same situation again.

Of course, the specific areas in which you use *Proactive Teaching* will vary with each child. To be successful in life, all children need to learn new skills and improve on the ones that they have had trouble with. You may want your foster child to learn new skills like *Table Etiquette* or *Answering the Telephone*. Or, you may want the child to get better at the skills that he or she has had difficulties with, like *Following Instructions* or *Accepting Consequences*. It all depends on the child and his or her specific skill deficits.

Many of the children who are placed in foster care have experienced too much criticism and too little success. They also have a lot of new rules and expectations to adjust to when they move to a new home. *Proactive Teaching* is an excellent tool to use when children first come into your home. It can help them learn and understand your rules and expectations, which may help them avoid problems and negative consequences.

**Proactive Teaching should be used when anxiety levels are low and emotions are under control.**

*Proactive Teaching* can be used any time *problem behaviors are not occurring,* when anxiety levels are low and emotions are under control. A comfortable, supportive, and relaxed environment can aid the learning process. This gives your foster child an opportunity to experience success without ever having to experience failure!

## Steps to Proactive Teaching

1. Describe the skill or behavior.
2. Give a reason.
3. Practice.

### 1. Describe the skill or behavior.

Before your foster child can do what you want, he or she must first know what you expect. Break the skill down into specific steps, and make sure the child understands. For example, if your foster daughter argues with her teachers about a consequence and gets sent to detention, you could teach her how to accept consequences from her teacher before she goes back to school the next day. You might say, *"Sharon, tomorrow at school if your teacher gives you a consequence for something, you should look at her, say 'Okay,' and don't argue. If she gives you instructions or suggestions on how to correct the situation, do what she says."*

### 2. Give a reason.

Foster children, like adults, benefit from knowing why they should act or do something a certain way. Reasons help a foster child understand why new skills and appropriate behaviors are useful and important. They also teach the child how inappropriate behaviors can be harmful. The best reasons, of course, are those that relate directly to the child's life. Simply telling foster children, *"Do it because I said so,"* is a command, not a reason. Foster children are more likely to use a skill long after they leave your home if they understand *why and how it will help them accomplish what is important to them.*

Sometimes it is difficult to come up with reasons that mean a lot to foster children at that time. But even if they don't immediately agree with what you are saying, at least they will know why you think using a certain behavior or skill is important. That means a great deal since giving reasons shows fairness and logic. Foster children are much more likely to comply with what you say when you give reasons. If reasons are personal to the child, he or she is more likely to accept what you are teaching. In the earlier example with Sharon, a reason for her to accept consequences from her teacher could be, *"When you yell or get upset with your teacher, you have to go to detention, and you can't spend time with your friends after school."*

## 3. Practice.

Knowing what to do and knowing how to do it are two different things. Any new skill, or skill that needs to be improved on, requires practice. You can tell your foster child how to ride a bicycle, but that does not mean that he or she can hop right on and take off. It takes practice to become good at almost anything.

Foster children occasionally are reluctant to practice, especially when they are learning a new skill. They may feel embarrassed, lack self-confidence, or think that it's a waste of time. The reality is that practice actually reduces embarrassment and raises the child's confidence in his or her abilities. It also helps the child to "generalize" the skill you're teaching; that means he or she learns how to use it in many situations. And your child will soon begin to understand how the skill will be worthwhile, not just now, but in the future.

If you are enthusiastic about practicing, your foster children will be more willing to practice. Encourage them and use a lot of praise for trying. Most practices should be fun yet realistic. This isn't the time to be super-serious; otherwise, the practice will become boring and tedious for you and your foster child.

In the earlier example with Sharon, you might have her practice the skill of *Accepting Consequences* by saying, *"Okay, Sharon, let's practice how to accept a consequence. Pretend I'm your teacher and I just gave you a consequence for talking in class. Show me what you'll do to accept the consequence. Okay?"*

Practice can be an enjoyable time with your foster children, especially when they understand that you are practicing because you care about them. Praise your foster child for doing things well, and encourage him or her to improve in areas that need

> **Practice raises the child's confidence in his or her abilities.**

improvement. Don't expect perfection the first time you practice. (Remember the idea of shaping?) For example, when you begin practicing with Sharon, maybe she takes a big breath to start calming down but continues to argue under her breath. By having her practice how to take a big breath and remain silent, she eventually will learn to stop

191

mumbling to herself and do what the teacher asks. If you make the practice enjoyable, and perhaps provide a reward for a good effort, Sharon will be more willing to practice several times. The more you practice the skill, the more likely Sharon will be to use it, if necessary, at school the next day.

If you are practicing a more complex skill or a difficult situation, such as *Resisting Peer Pressure* (saying "No" to using drugs), your foster child needs to understand that the "real" situation may turn out very differently. Explain to your foster child that you are practicing possible ways to handle a situation and that the outcome won't always be the same. This is no different from what we go through in our daily lives. We know that a certain way of dealing with one person won't work with another person. As a Foster Parent, you cannot ensure your foster child's success in every situation; you can only improve the odds. Your foster children will learn that every situation is different, but they won't be defenseless. You will help them learn more and better ways to solve problems, until they have several solutions to choose from.

After finishing any teaching situation, encourage the child to use the skill in real situations in the future. Also, praise the child for paying attention, working hard, and taking time to practice. As a child gets better at using a skill, you may have to use only one or two steps of *Proactive Teaching* when reviewing the skill.

## Opportunities for Proactive Teaching

As we mentioned earlier, *Proactive Teaching* can be very helpful when you are trying to help a foster child adjust to a new home, school, and neighborhood. Here are some other opportunities for using *Proactive Teaching:*

- **When teaching or discussing house rules.** This is a critical part of every foster child's introduction to a new home.

- **When teaching basic safety.** Your foster child may not be familiar with certain potential hazards in your neighborhood, such as traffic, lakes, or pets. He or she also may be unfamiliar with appliances or special recreational equipment.

- **When discussing or planning home visits.** *Proactive Teaching* can be used before a foster child goes on a home visit or to visit other relatives. For example, if a foster child arrived at your home and you were told that the child had difficulties with the skill of *Following Instructions* and *Accepting Criticism* during home visits, you and the child could do some extra practices with these skills before the child's next visit. This will help the foster child focus on those skills and prepare for a more successful visit.

## Examples of Proactive Teaching

**Situation:** Robbie, your 6-year-old foster son, is about

to go outside to play; he sometimes doesn't come inside when you call him.

**1. Describe the skill or behavior.**

Foster Parent: *"Robbie, let's talk about following instructions. When I call you to come in for dinner, please let me know that you heard me, then pick up your toys right away before coming in."*

**2. Give a reason.**

Foster Parent: *"If you follow instructions and come in right away, I'll be more likely to give you permission to play after dinner."*

**3. Practice.**

Foster Parent: *"Let's pretend I've just called you in. What are you going to say and do?"*

Robbie: *"I'm going to say 'Okay,' put my toys away, and come into the kitchen."*

Foster Parent: *"Great! Nice job of **following instructions**. Now run and have fun. Remember to come in right away when I call."*

**Situation:** Your teenage foster daughter, Michelle, wants to spend an overnight visit with her family, but her caseworker did not approve the visit. Michelle wants to call the caseworker to ask her to reconsider.

**1. Describe the skill or behavior.**

Foster Parent: *"I know you really want your caseworker to change her mind, but she may not. Let's talk about how you should **disagree appropriately** in case that happens. If she says 'No,' you need to say*

*'Okay' and calmly ask for a reason if you don't understand. If you disagree, you can bring it up with her next week when she comes for a visit."*

**2. Give a reason.**

Foster Parent: *"If you show her that you are learning to **disagree appropriately,** she may be more willing to let you spend more time with your family in the future because she will be more confident that the visits with your family will go better."*

**3. Practice.**

Foster Parent: *"Let's pretend that you just asked to go on the overnight visit and your caseworker said 'No.' How would you **disagree appropriately?** "*

Michelle: *"I'm going to say 'Okay,' and ask her why she said 'No.' If I don't like her reason, I can talk with her more about it next week when she comes to see me."*

Foster Parent: *"Very good. I think she will be very impressed that you can handle a difficult situation."*

## Proactive Prompts

Experience adds skills. Eventually, when your foster child is faced with situations where he or she can use the same skill, you may just have to provide a reminder – a **proactive prompt**. For example, let's say that you have practiced accepting consequences from a teacher with your foster daughter, and she is just about to leave for school. A proactive prompt might sound like:

*"Sharon, do you remember the steps to **accepting consequences** that we practiced last night? (Sharon says, "Yes.") Great! Remember to use those steps with your teacher if you have to."*

The purpose of a proactive prompt is to get your foster child focused on what you have practiced so that she can use the skill when needed. Your praise and encouragement during the whole *Proactive Teaching* sequence will help your foster child remember to use important skills when they are most needed.

## Summary

*Proactive Teaching* is a valuable tool for both Foster Parents and foster children. By using it with your foster children, you can help them prepare for unfamiliar situations and promote gradual behavior changes in areas where they may be having problems. *Proactive Teaching* can increase your foster children's self-esteem by showing them that they can learn how to change their behaviors and avoid problems. And, perhaps most importantly, *Proactive Teaching* allows you and your foster child to work toward goals together. Taking the time to be with your foster children and showing them that you care helps improve relationships, and that benefits the whole family.

# CHAPTER 13

# Giving
# Effective Praise

When foster children come to your home, do they feel good about themselves? Can they identify their talents and strengths? Do they think they are good learners? Are they calm and self-confident?

In most cases, the answer is probably "No." Many children going into a new foster home feel adrift and alone. They may feel responsible for the break-up of their families and overwhelmed by the task of trying to make it better. They may think they are "bad kids," deserving whatever bad treatment they get. Or, they may think they are stupid and unlovable. Emotional abuse is one of the most damaging types of abuse; its legacy is that you believe you are not worthy of being cared for or loved. How can Foster Parents begin to replace their foster child's negative self-image with something positive and meaningful?

One way is to consistently and sincerely praise a child for the things he or she does well. Praise is nourishment for the foster child's mind and self-esteem. In the Girls and

Boys Town model of care, we use a powerful tool called *Effective Praise* to help children develop or restore a positive self-image.

## Focus on the Positive

Praise is not a new concept; everyone is familiar with it. But many people don't use it as often as they should. Why? One of the reasons is that we have been "conditioned" by society to focus on the negative things people do or the negative parts of a situation. It is easy to see what people do wrong. We usually overlook or don't notice positive behaviors when things are going the way we want. But as soon as things start going badly, we notice and often respond with criticism or correction.

Unfortunately, some untrained Foster Parents tend to focus on the negative with their foster children. It's easy for them to see their kids' mistakes and shortcomings. And when the Foster Parents do give praise, the children are so unfamiliar with it that they don't believe the compliments at first. They may reply, *"Oh yeah, sure"* or *"You are just saying that because you have to."*

As we've mentioned in previous chapters, strong relationships are vital to providing effective teaching and helping children change their behaviors. One way to build and strengthen your relationship with your foster child is through the use of *Effective Praise*. Praising your foster child sincerely and specifically will not only increase his or her positive behaviors, but also will make you feel better about your job as a Foster Parent.

## Praise Works!

Girls and Boys Town has found one thing to be true time and time again: **Praise works wonders.** When Foster Parents use praise consistently, foster children change dramatically. When Foster Parents "zero in" on as many positive things as possible, foster children begin to feel better about themselves, and their behavior improves.

Some people say that they praise their children but it just doesn't seem to work. Most of the time, though, the praise is given only for outstanding achievements or momentous occasions. They forget to look for and praise the little things kids do. After they learn the importance of praising small improvements, and actually do it, they begin to notice many positive changes in their children's behavior. This is not a coincidence: Praise works!

> **When Foster Parents use praise consistently, foster children change dramatically.**

Some Foster Parents ask, *"Why should I praise my foster children for something that they're supposed to do?"* The following questions can provide an answer: *"Do you like being recognized for the things you do well, regardless of whether you're supposed to do them? Do you like to hear your boss tell you what a good job you're doing?"* Most Foster Parents say, *"Of course,"* and then add, *"and I wouldn't mind hearing it a little more often."* Enough said. *All* people – kids and adults – like to hear praise for things they do well. And remember: Your foster child probably hasn't heard much praise. Think of him or her as a plant deprived of water and sunlight. *Effective Praise* is the nourishment the foster child needs to bloom and grow into a healthy, productive individual.

## When to Praise

When praising your foster children, it helps to look closely at three areas:

1. Things your foster children already do well (and maybe you take for granted).
2. Improvements, even small improvements, in problem areas.
3. Positive attempts at new skills.

This means praising your foster child for following everyday instructions like coming home from school on time, cleaning his or her room, or turning off the lights. He or she is more likely to continue to follow instructions because you took the time to notice and praise.

**Praise any step in the right direction.**

If your foster child tries hard to learn something new, praise the effort. Remember that shaping involves praising any step in the right direction. Learning a skill requires learning small parts of it, then putting all of the steps together. When your own child was learning to walk, you probably praised each and every improvement – from the first time he or she stood alone, to taking that first awkward step, to finally putting a series of steps together. When foster children first come to your home, there is so much for them to learn. You may have many expectations for them that you tend to take for granted – eating at the table as a family, getting up on time for school, or sleeping in pajamas. If you praise their positive attempts to learn or try a new skill and other improvements, their enthusiasm and effort can carry over to other areas. Seize every opportunity to recognize positive attempts to learn.

## Steps of Effective Praise

The easiest way to praise someone is to say things like *"Fantastic!", "Great!",* or *"Keep up the good work!"* This is a good start, but you can take it a little further to make sure your foster child receives a clear message. That's why we make a distinction between praise in general and *Effective Praise.*

*Effective Praise* allows you to do the following:
- **Recognize your foster children** sincerely and enthusiastically for the progress they are making.
- **Specifically describe** what they did that you liked.
- **Give a reason** why you liked it.

In Chapter 5, "Setting Expectations and Sending Clear Messages," we discussed a framework to use when teaching to your foster children. This is the basis for *Effective Praise.* Here are the steps:

1. **Show your approval.** Smiling and giving a pat on the back are enthusiastic ways to show approval. A brief praise statement such as *"Great job!"* also is effective.

2. **Describe the positive behavior/Label the skill.** Give clear, specific descriptions of the behavior(s) and skill your foster child did well.

3. **Give a reason.** Tell the child how using the skill can help him or her, or how it can help others.

4. **(Optional) Give a reward.** You can give a reward (or positive consequence), depending on the situation and the behavior or skill the child used.

Let's look at an example of *Effective Praise:*

**Situation:** Your teenage foster son called to tell you where he is and that he will be late.

1. **Show your approval.**

   *"Thanks for calling me, Tony."*

2. **Describe the positive behavior/Label the skill.**

   *"I'm really glad you're checking in and letting me know where you are and why you'll be a little late."*

3. **Give a reason.**

   *"That shows responsibility and lets me know that I can trust you."*

4. **(Optional) Give a reward.**

   *"For checking in, you can stay out an extra 15 minutes the next time you go out."* (You could save this step for

when Tony gets home. That way, he gets praise two times.)

In this brief scenario, your foster child learned specifically what he did right (checking in) and why it was so important (it shows responsibility). By recognizing his appropriate behavior, you increased the likelihood that he will call you the next time he's in the same situation.

Let's look more closely at these relatively easy steps and see why they are important.

## 1. Show your approval.

Foster children are like the rest of us. They not only like to hear nice things said about them, but they'll also work harder to get more praise. As mentioned earlier, many foster children may have been emotionally neglected or abused. They are really starved for someone to notice them and their abilities. When you combine a sign of your approval with specific praise, it's that much more meaningful.

There are numerous words that you can use to show your approval, and, for goodness sake, show a little excitement! *"Awesome! Terrific! Wow! You're right on target! I'm impressed! Super! Amazing! That's great! Wonderful! Magnificent! Excellent!"* (Doesn't it make you feel better just saying these words?)

There also are numerous actions that convey your approval to your foster children: Winking or smiling at them. Giving them a "thumbs up" or an "A-Okay" sign. Ruffling their hair. Giving them "five." Nodding your head. Clapping for them. And when you know that it's okay to do so, hugging them.

Showing your approval lets foster children know that you're excited about what they're doing. Every foster child gives us something to be happy about. Every foster child does something that deserves praise. Make sure you recognize it, and, most of all, tell them.

## 2. Describe the positive behavior/Label the skill.

After you have given a praise statement, describe the specific behaviors you liked. Make sure your foster children understand what they did so that they can repeat the behavior in the future. Give them clear messages. Praise what you just saw or heard your foster child do well: *"Sue, thanks for washing the dishes and helping me put the leftovers away,"* or *"Eddie, I'm glad you washed your hands after you went to the bathroom."*

Along with specifically describing the behavior, you should also identify the skill: *"Sue, thanks for cleaning the dishes and helping me put the leftovers away. You did a nice job of **following instructions.**"* When you identify the skill, you're helping your foster child to understand the importance of his or her behavior, not just in this specific situation, but overall. In time, he or she begins to see that *Following Instructions* is not just about helping with the dishes, but is important at school, work, on the soccer field, and in thousands of other situations.

Remember to use words your foster children understand. Make the statements brief and to the point. Just let your foster child know what was done well.

### 3. Give a reason.

Children want to know why they should use certain behaviors or skills. Giving a reason as part of your teaching explains to children how they or others will benefit from a behavior or skill. When foster children first come into your home, it is best to use reasons that deal with short-term effects. As foster children develop and begin to make the new skill they have learned part of their everyday lives, you can use reasons that point out long-term benefits. This is also a good time to use reasons that show how the youths' behaviors can help others. This helps foster children learn empathy for other people and understand that their actions affect others.

Let's use this example to see how these different types of reasons can be used: Your teenager voluntarily cleans up the family room before guests come over.

In order to explain why that behavior is helpful, you could use one of the following reasons:

- *"Since you **volunteered** to help out, I'll have time to take you over to your friend's house when you want to go. I don't know if I would have had time if you hadn't helped."* (Benefits youth; short term)
- *"**Volunteering** to help others is a real plus. If you do that on the job, your boss is more likely to give you a raise."* (Benefits youth; long term)

- *"**Volunteering** to clean the family room really saved me a lot of time. Now I have time to get everything finished before guests come over."* (Benefits others)

Giving your foster child a reason for using a certain behavior shows the relationship between the behavior and the consequences or outcomes. Unfortunately, most foster children have not been taught this relationship. A child may say that his teacher gave him poor grades "because she didn't like me," rather than because he was frequently absent or didn't turn in his homework. Reasons should be brief, believable, and age-appropriate.

Here are some more examples of how reasons can be given to kids. (The skill being praised follows the reason.)

- *"It's important to answer the phone politely because it may be your mother or a friend."* (Skill: Telephone Skills)

- *"It's important to tell your teacher when you don't have your homework done because it shows that you're willing to take responsibility."* (Skill: Accepting Responsibility)

- *"It's important to be on time to see your caseworker because she has set aside time for you, and we want her to know we appreciate it."* (Skill: Time Management)

- *"Picking up your things is important because people won't step on them and break them."* (Skill: Following Instructions)

206

## 4. (Optional) Give a reward.

Occasionally, you may want to add a fourth step – giving a reward (or positive consequence) – when you use *Effective Praise*. When you are especially pleased with a certain behavior or when your foster child has made a big improvement in a certain area, you can reward him or her with a special privilege.

Rewards can be big or small; that's up to you. If possible, give rewards that are related to the type of behavior you want to encourage. Rewards also will help make your praise more reinforcing over time.

Many children coming into foster care feel lonesome and homesick at times. They also have missed out on spending time with adults who put the child's needs first, so spending extra time together doing simple activities is one of the biggest rewards you can give. It also is important for that child's care.

Here are some more examples of how *Effective Praise* can be used:

1. **Show approval.**

   *"Michael, that's great!"*

2. **Describe positive behavior/Label the skill.**

   *"You followed instructions and tied your tennis shoes all by yourself!"*

3. **Give a reason.**

   *"Now you won't have to wait for me to do it for you."*

1. **Show approval.**

   *"I'm so proud of you!"*

2. **Describe positive behavior/Label the skill.**

   *"You took responsibility and did your homework before watching TV."*

3. **Give a reason.**

   *"Now, you won't have to do it late at night."*

4. **Give a reward.**

   *"You're welcome to make some popcorn while you watch the movie."*

1. **Show approval.**

   *"Kathy, what a nice job!"*

2. **Describe positive behavior/Label the skill.**

   *"You asked for help and told me you and Susan were having trouble sharing your toys. You told me before any hitting started."*

3. **Give a reason.**

   *"When you come to me for help right away, neither of you have to go to time-out."*

## Summary

Foster Parents who use *Effective Praise* will make a lasting impact on their foster children. As you use this teaching method, you will find yourself being more positive about your foster children. Foster children, in turn, are more positive about you. With *Effective Praise,* everyone wins.

# CHAPTER 14

# Staying Calm

One of the biggest challenges Foster Parents face is staying calm when dealing with their foster children's problem behaviors. During these times, many foster children can become upset and angry – and so can the Foster Parents. When kids are upset or angry, they can be sarcastic, defiant, rebellious, and even aggressive. Foster Parents must prepare themselves for these times and learn how to keep their cool.

You will get upset, angry, and frustrated with kids. It's only natural, so expect it to happen. It's impossible, even unhealthy, not to experience these basic human emotions. However, "blowing your top" over your foster child's misbehavior will only make the situation worse. Adults who have many confrontations with their foster children frequently reinforce inappropriate behaviors and cause more con-

> **Foster Parents must learn how to keep their cool.**

frontations to occur. Research has shown that a family's interaction style – especially in dysfunctional families – may serve as basic training for aggressive behavior in children (Patterson, Dishion, & Bank, 1984). The way we look at it, anger is only one letter away from "danger." Girls and Boys Town's experience shows that teaching is much more effective when adults can stay calm and control their angry responses.

## What Makes You Angry?

Knowing what makes you upset or angry is the first step in learning how to stay calm and control your anger. Since your actions greatly influence how an angry child responds to what you say or do, be aware of your actions. That way, you can avoid behaviors that might trigger a negative response from your foster child. This will decrease the chances of having unnecessary confrontations with the child.

When adults are angry, they may use many negative behaviors: yelling, cursing, hitting something, or throwing something. Some adults may even hit children in a fit of anger. As discussed in Chapter 4, "Creating a Safe Environment," Girls and Boys Town policy (and most states) prohibits physical discipline of foster children. However, many untrained Foster Parents are convinced that their angry responses work. And they are partially right; such responses can temporarily stop a problem behavior. But in the end, all children really learn is that yelling, hitting, or throwing or kicking things are acceptable ways to respond when they are upset or angry.

As a role model you can help change your foster child's inappropriate expressions of anger and frustration by modeling and teaching healthier ways to deal with strong emotions. The Girls and Boys Town foster care program helps Foster Parents learn how to stay calm in tense situations. When Foster Parents stay calm, they report the following:

- The child's temper tantrum or problem behavior stops sooner and is less severe.

- The Foster Parent feels better about the way he or she handled the situation.

One Foster Parent told us, *"You know, that 'staying calm' thing really works. Before, I'd get mad at something my foster son did and lose my temper, and he'd run away. I didn't handle these situations very well.* Now that I've figured out that my getting angry was what caused him to run away and I've learned how to stay calm, we are able to work things out without him running away."

**Anger is only one letter away from "danger."**

Of course, staying calm was just one of the effective changes this Foster Parent made in his parenting style. But becoming aware of the importance of staying calm was the first step. He learned that his anger got in the way of how he cared for his foster son. As the foster father learned to remain calm, he was able to put his parenting skills to work. This led to a dramatic, positive change in the relationship between this man and his foster son.

## Calming Down

For many Foster Parents, staying calm isn't easy at first. They have to work at it. The best way to stay calm when working with a foster child is for Foster Parents to come up with a plan or strategy. Here's how some Foster Parents report they calm down during tense situations:

- *"I count to 10, very slowly. I concentrate on doing that regardless of what my foster son is yelling."*

- *"I put my hands in my pockets. I tend to be really demonstrative with my hands, especially when I'm angry. Before I learned to do this, I think my foster daughter thought I was going to hit her. I wasn't, but she viewed my behavior as a threat."*

- *"I sit down. If I'm standing, I begin to tremble. Sitting calms me for some reason. I can still tell my foster child what he's doing wrong, but I say it a lot more calmly."*

- *"I take a deep breath and let it out slowly. For me, this kind of serves as a safety valve. It's like I'm letting steam out of my body."*

- *"I just leave the situation for a while. I go to another room until I can calm myself down. I figure that if my kid's that mad, taking a little time to regain my control won't hurt anything. I can deal with it a lot better that way. Sometimes, she even calms down by the time I get back."*

- *"I'll talk to my spouse. By talking about the situation, I can go back in and deal with it more calmly."*

These are suggestions on how to calm down when you're already angry. An even better strategy is to recognize when you're beginning to get angry and start the calming down process right away. All people have little signals that warn them when they are starting to become angry. Recognizing these signals allows you to think before you act. When you're calm, it's much easier to find a solution to a problem. Here are some physical warning signs of anger:

- Tensing muscles
- Sweating
- Speaking faster and/or louder
- Feeling flushed
- Grinding or clenching teeth
- Pounding heart
- Quivering lips
- Ringing in the ears
- Trembling or shaking
- Clenching fists

Now, let's take a look at how recognizing these signals can help you stay calm in tense situations with your foster child. The following example combines these three elements:

1. A foster child's problem behaviors.
2. A Foster Parent's early warning signals.

3.  A way of staying calm that works for the Foster Parent.

## Example

Travis talked back to his Foster Parent and refused to go to bed *(child's problem behaviors)*. The Foster Parent started to feel her heart pound *(warning signal),* so she took a deep breath and let it out slowly before she began teaching *(way to stay calm)*.

# More Tips on Staying Calm

Learning to control your negative responses will take some time and practice. Here are some tips that have helped other Foster Parents:

**Don't take what your foster child says personally.**

This may be very difficult when your foster child is calling you names or cursing at you. But, remember that the child has yet to master the skills necessary to deal with his or her anger or frustration. Don't react when a child calls you names, accuses you of being a rotten Foster Parent, or negatively compares you to other caretakers with whom the child has lived. Simply let these negative, angry comments bounce off you. Instead of getting angry yourself, remember that you can use consequences like the loss of a privilege or time-out to deal with the situation in a constructive way.

**"Take five."**

Instead of saying something out of anger or frustration, take five minutes to calm down, think about what is happening, and plan how you are going to proceed. It is remarkable how a "cooling off" period like this can help a person regain control and put things in perspective. In addition, it is more likely that you will choose a fair and reasonable consequence for the child's misbehavior.

**Be aware of your behavior.**

It is important to use a calm voice tone and appropriate language. Also, it's a good idea to stand an arm's length away, especially when your foster child is really angry or upset. Match your foster child's general posture (sit down if the child is sitting), and don't use gestures that the child might see as threatening or as a challenge (pointing your finger at the child, clenching your fists, putting your hands on your hips, and so on).

**Focus on the child's behavior instead of the child's motive.**

Don't try to figure out why a child is misbehaving; instead, deal with the way he or she is behaving. It is important that the child understands that you are frustrated or upset only with the behavior, and that you don't think that he or she is a bad person. After the problem is resolved, you can take time to think about what happened and why, and discuss it with your foster child if necessary. During the discussion, be careful not to bring up old issues and appear to be nagging or badgering the child.

**If appropriate, say you're sorry.**

If you get angry and say or do something you regret, tell the child you're sorry. This teaches your foster children how to behave when they make a mistake. Apologize, say what you did wrong, and tell the child what you're going to do differently next time. Some Foster Parents think that by apologizing, they lose some of their parental control. We have found that apologizing helps foster children realize that everyone, adults included, makes mistakes. When you model apologizing, your foster children learn to say they are sorry much quicker and more often to you and others for mistakes and misbehaviors.

**Use an appropriate voice tone.**

There are times when you will want to be firm and use a no-nonsense voice tone. During these times, you should use words that give specific descriptions. Do not make judgments or express feelings. Staying calm means that you don't overreact to misbehavior in an angry, aggressive manner. So, don't yell at your foster child; it will only escalate an already tense situation.

## Summary

Providing effective care means staying calm even during difficult and tense situations. It isn't always easy to stay calm. However, your ability to do so will make your teaching more effective and will eventually make interactions with your foster child less confrontational. Modeling calm behaviors also shows your foster child how you expect him or her to behave in difficult situations.

Remember these six guidelines the next time you are angry or upset with your foster child:

1. Stay calm.

2. Be aware of your own behavior.

3. Identify what makes you angry.

4. Know what you are going to say and do.

5. Control negative responses, and deal with them quickly.

6. Remember that your self-control is a key to staying calm and defusing potential problems before they can escalate.

# CHAPTER 15

# Correcting Misbehavior

Foster children often will try to test the limits of their Foster Parents. Testing limits means pushing the rules to see how much and what kind of behavior Foster Parents will allow until they respond. In many respects, this is healthy. Testing limits is one way kids learn, grow, and find out about the world around them. Foster children test limits so they can find out how their new family functions. Testing limits also helps them learn about the boundaries between grownups and children, how these boundaries are set, who sets them, and the type of consequences that are used when someone abides by or violates the boundaries. However, when foster children continually misbehave in order to test the limits set by Foster Parents, it can cause problems for the whole family.

*Corrective Teaching* is the method Girls and Boys Town has developed to deal with the problems Foster Parents face when their foster children misbehave. It is a proven, effective teaching process that helps children learn new, appropriate behaviors that can replace inappropriate ones.

Problem behaviors vary from child to child. With your foster child, what behaviors aggravate you the most? When do these behaviors take place?

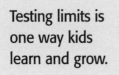

**Testing limits is one way kids learn and grow.**

do these behaviors take place? Where do these behaviors take place? How often do they take place? The answers to these questions usually lead you to the behaviors that cause your child the most problems. **The more clearly you specify a child's problem behaviors, the more likely you are to find a solution to them.**

Here's a sample of some frustrating problem behaviors that Foster Parents have shared with us:

- *"I always have to ask two or three times whenever I want my foster child to do something."*

- *"It seems like my foster children argue all the time. And about the dumbest things. They just pick, pick, pick at one another until one of them gets mad."*

- *"She gets so angry sometimes. She threatens to run away, and she yells at me when I confront her about her lying. I worry that I'm not up to the job of being a Foster Parent."*

- *"I can't get him to help with the dishes unless I threaten to take away a privilege."*

- *"When I ask my foster son about his homework, he says it's done or he left it at school. Sooner or later, he gets a negative note from his teacher at school saying it's not done."*

- *"He argues with me about everything. I can't remember the last time I asked him to do something and he actually just went and did it."*

One Foster Parent summed up the frustration many Foster Parents feel when she said, *"What can I do? I've had it! I feel like all I do is yell or punish him all day. He thinks I'm a monster, but I can't get him to do a thing!"* Like most concerned Foster Parents, this woman was looking for a constructive, effective way to respond to her foster child's misbehavior. *Corrective Teaching* is the answer.

## What Is Corrective Teaching?

*Corrective Teaching* is a five-step process that combines clear messages with consequences and practice. This helps you respond to problem behaviors by teaching children new skills. You use *Corrective Teaching* when your foster children are not following instructions or when they are displaying any inappropriate behavior. This includes times when they are:

- Doing something you've asked them not to do.
- Not doing something you've asked them to do.
- Doing something that could harm them or others.

## Steps to Corrective Teaching

Here are the steps for *Corrective Teaching.* An explanation of each step and how it works follows.

1. Stop the problem behavior.
2. Give a consequence.

3. Describe what you want/Label the skill.

4. Give a reason.

5. Practice what you want.

## 1. Stop the problem behavior.

One of the most effective ways to get a child's attention is by making an empathy statement using a calm voice. Your foster child is more likely to listen and want to hear what you have to say if you speak in a pleasant voice and express sincere concern. It is helpful to try to have your foster child look at you, but you can continue the teaching process even if the child doesn't. As we have mentioned, you must be aware of your physical behaviors. Your foster child may perceive actions such as pointing your finger, putting your hands on your hips, or getting too close to him or her as aggressive behaviors.

A calm, reassuring approach should always be used when you begin teaching; otherwise, your foster child may come to view you as a person who is unpleasant to be around, quick to criticize, and slow to appreciate or understand the child's frustrations. A calm, caring approach will help you build a relationship with your foster child, even when he or she is having difficulties.

Once you have your foster child's attention, you can give clear instructions about how you want him or her to stop the problem behavior. This may be as simple as saying, *"Please sit down"* or *"Please lower your voice."*

It also is very helpful to briefly describe your foster child's negative behavior(s) before you continue the teaching process. This lets him or her know exactly what behavior(s) you are addressing with your teaching.

If your foster child continues to refuse to follow your instructions or starts using more severe or aggressive behaviors, you can use another teaching method called *Teaching Self-Control* (This teaching method is explained in the next chapter.) **Corrective Teaching is used to help children stop a misbehavior and learn alternative behaviors when they are responding fairly quickly to your instructions and teaching.**

## 2. Give a consequence.

Options for consequences should be discussed with your foster child when he or she first arrives at your home. The important thing to remember is to give a consequence that is closely related to the inappropriate behavior. That way, your foster child knows that the consequence is a direct result of his or her action.

In addition, give children a chance to earn back part of the consequence. This occurs if your foster child is attentive and works to make up for the misbehavior, and you are pleased with the attempt. This is called **positive correction.**

How much of a consequence should children be able to earn back? A good rule to follow is no more than *half* of what they lost. For example, during *Corrective Teaching,* you could take away one hour of TV time from your foster son and foster daughter because they were arguing. After you finish teaching, both children apologize and say they will work together to wash the dishes. If they cooperate, they could earn back up to 30 minutes of the TV time they lost. Allowing children to earn a positive consequence for working on the problem is an effective way to teach them that they can make up for mistakes or misbehaviors.

Many foster children give up too easily on trying to correct their behavior. They may feel as though they can't do anything right. It is important to remember that children who have experienced severe or unreasonable punishments in the past may feel powerless. **Giving your foster children an opportunity to earn back part of a consequence helps motivate them to not give up and, as a result, helps them accomplish their goals sooner.**

Some Foster Parents may be uncomfortable with the idea of letting children earn back some of their lost privileges. They may be concerned that the child will view them as being "weak" or "easy." In reality, children frequently view Foster Parents as "fair" and "willing to help with problems" when they are given a chance to earn back some of what was lost. So an added bonus of positive correction is that it strengthens your relationship with your foster children.

Finally, it is often difficult to remain objective when determining an appropriate consequence for a child's misbehavior. This can be especially true when the behavior is aggressive, repetitive, or harmful to others. Consider the following factors when deciding on a fair consequence:

1. How often does the problem behavior occur?
2. How long does the problem behavior last?

3. How disruptive is the problem behavior?

4. How dangerous is the problem behavior?

5. Where and at what time does the problem behavior usually occur?

### 3. Describe what you want/Label the skill.

Describing the behavior and labeling the skill you want your foster child to use the next time a similar problem arises reinforces consistency in your teaching. This is true because you will be describing a skill (and its steps) that should have already been introduced during *Proactive Teaching*. Specifically describing the skill's steps and reinforcing the child when he or she uses them correctly makes it more likely that the child will use the skill more frequently and consistently. You also can teach your foster child how to apply the skill to the situation at hand and others like it. This helps the child learn how to use the skill with other situations and people. (This is called generalization.)

### 4. Give a reason.

It is important to help your foster child understand how inappropriate behaviors can cause problems and how changing those behaviors can help him or her. For example, you might tell a child who doesn't share with others that other children will not want to play with him because of that behavior; you might add that he will have more friends if he shares toys while playing. Remember that using reasons your foster child can easily understand will help motivate him or her to learn new, appropriate behaviors to replace problem behaviors.

Be clear and brief, and do not give too many reasons at one time; that way it won't seem like you are lecturing. Also, when possible, make the reason personal to the youth; it will have a greater impact. For example, *Accepting Criticism* is an important skill for a child who wants to make a sports team. If appropriate, use this as part of the reason you give for learning that skill.

### 5. Practice what you want.

Foster children are more likely to begin using a skill if they practice the skill at the end of *Corrective Teaching*. Practice is most effective when it's brief and pleasant for the child; using praise and positive humor helps accomplish this. Practice also helps you determine how effective your teaching is. By watching your foster child practice, you can determine whether he or she is learning the skill or needs extra teaching.

## Using Corrective Teaching

Now let's look at two examples of how the five steps of Corrective Teaching can be used to help correct problem behaviors.

### Examples

**Situation:** A Foster Parent hears two youngsters argue about who gets to play with some new blocks. The Foster Parent then observes his foster son knock over a tower of blocks that the other child has built.

**1. Stop the problem behavior.**

- Use empathy.
- Calmly get his attention.
- Give a clear instruction.
- Describe what happened or is happening.

*"Michael, please come sit down. Thank you. I know you're upset right now. I just saw you knock over the tower of blocks that Tony had built."*

**2. Deliver a consequence.**

- Relate it to the problem behavior.

*"For knocking over Tony's tower, you will not be able to play with the blocks the rest of the day. But if you work with me and practice the skill of **sharing**, you might be able to play with the blocks later."*

**3. Describe what you want/Label the skill.**

- Be specific.
- Describe the skill you want the child to practice.

*"Michael, when you share with others, you shouldn't get upset if you're asked to share. You should take turns and play fair, and if the other person thanks you, say, 'You're welcome.'"*

**4. Give a reason.**

- Relate it to the foster child.

*"**Sharing with others** is important because then other kids will be more likely to share their toys with you."*

**5. Practice what you want.**

- Keep it brief.
- Praise during practice.

  *"Now here's a chance for you to show me that you can share with others. You've done a good job of listening so far, Michael. Okay, pretend that you think Tony has taken your blocks. What would you do?"*

  (Michael correctly uses the steps of *Sharing*.)

  *"That was great, Michael! You used each step of sharing. Since you were calm and did such a good job practicing, you can play with the blocks for one hour after dinner."*

**Situation:** Your 14-year-old foster daughter asks if she can go to a friend's house with three other girls. You tell her "No" because she hasn't done her homework. She begins to argue and calls you unfair.

**1. Stop the problem behavior.**

- Use empathy.
- Calmly get her attention.
- Give a clear instruction.
- Describe what happened or is happening.

  *"It's hard when you don't get to do what you want, Sadie. Would you please come over and sit down at the table. Thanks for coming over. Now, after you asked me to go to Tia's and I said 'No,' you began arguing and calling me unfair."*

**2. Give a consequence.**

- Relate it to the problem behavior.

*"For not accepting 'No' for an answer, you can't use the phone tonight to talk with your friends. But if you hang in there and practice with me, you'll have a chance to earn some of that time back."*

**3. Describe what you want/Label the skill.**

- Be specific.

- Describe the skill you want the child to practice .

*"The next time you're told 'No,' remember to look at the person, say 'Okay,' stay calm, and if you disagree, talk to the person about it later."*

**4. Give a reason.**

- Relate it to the foster child.

*"If you can accept 'No' answers calmly, it will show that you have control of your emotions and, if possible, the person is more likely to say 'Yes' next time."*

**5. Practice what you want.**

- Keep it brief.

- Praise during practice.

Foster Parent: *"Let's pretend that I just told you that you can't go to a movie with Jennifer. What should you do?"*

Sadie: *"I'd look at you, say 'Okay,' and stay calm."*

Foster Parent: *"Nice job! Thanks for practicing so*

*well. You've earned back 30 minutes of phone time. Why don't you do your homework now, and when you're finished, you can use the phone."*

Now that you've seen how *Corrective Teaching* can work, practice it with your spouse or another adult until you feel confident in your ability to do the steps. Practice leads to confidence, and confidence leads to success.

## Tips for Using Corrective Teaching

Here are some important things to keep in mind when using Corrective Teaching:

**Remain calm.**

As you learned in the last chapter, this is easier said than done. Foster Parents tell us this is one of the most important pieces to successful teaching. Sometimes, foster children misbehave so often that Foster Parents respond angrily. Or the behavior itself is so annoying that Foster Parents react abruptly or negatively. Remember to stop and think about what you need to do.

**Respect your foster child's privacy.**

Most of you probably can remember being disciplined as a child in front of your brothers or sisters, or even worse, in front of your friends. Being embarrassed made it pretty hard to concentrate on what you were being corrected for and why. The same is true for foster children who already may feel that they are different from other children. Once you have stopped the misbehavior, do *Corrective Teaching* in a place where there won't be an audience. You are much more likely to have your foster child's undivided attention and preserve your relationship when you respect his or her privacy.

**Stick to one issue.**
Most children are very good at getting adults sidetracked. Some foster children can get Foster Parents so far off the topic that they forget what it is. Statements like the following are particularly effective in doing this:

*"I hate you!"*

*"My parents didn't make me do that. They're nice."*

*"I don't want to talk about that, and you can't make me!"*

*"You can take away anything you want. I just don't care!"*

*"I can't wait until I'm out of this foster home. I thought you were supposed to help me!"*

Certainly, these types of comments can go straight to your heart. We've all wanted to remind our children or foster children of all the nice things we do for them or to prove what good parents we are. But stick with what you want to teach. When foster children bring up other issues as they are being corrected, they are usually trying to avoid earning negative consequences. Don't get sidetracked into a meaningless discussion brought up by an upset child. *This is very important:* Let your foster children know that if they really want to talk about other topics, they can bring them up after the main issue is resolved and they have accepted their consequences.

**Be consistent.**

Being consistent means using *Corrective Teaching* to address inappropriate behaviors every time they occur. (This consistency also applies to using *Effective Praise* to recognize positive behaviors.) Many foster children come from chaotic homes, and the benefits of living with Foster Parents who provide consistency are enormous. These benefits might not be evident right away. During the first few weeks, many foster children find it difficult to adjust to an environment where a caregiver responds to almost every behavior. But we strongly encourage you to stay the course; the foster child eventually will begin to test limits less and less and to respond positively to your teaching.

One of the benefits for children in foster care is that house rules and consequences (both positive and negative) are consistently applied every day. When foster children do cooperate with you, use *Effective Praise* and some creative rewards. It's important to provide stability in your foster children's lives. The more consistent you are, the more consistent your foster children will be.

**Be flexible.**

Just when we tell you to be consistent, we throw you a curve and talk about flexibility. Flexibility means consistently using *Corrective Teaching* but varying the way you use it. As you get to know your foster child better, you will learn what teaching style and what rewards and negative consequences work best. For example, if you think your foster child will learn more if you put the consequence at the end of *Corrective Teaching,* then give it a try. However, it is important to use all the steps. Each step has a purpose, and together they make *Corrective Teaching* a powerful teaching tool.

There are a few essential points to make with this approach: At first, learn and use the teaching steps the way they're presented, then adapt them to meet the individual needs of your foster child. For example, brief and specific teaching would work best with very young foster children because they tend to have short attention spans. Older children, who typically have longer attention spans, are better able to process longer, more detailed teaching.

## Summary

Foster Parents who take the time to use each of the steps of *Corrective Teaching* are amazed at how easy it becomes and how it helps to change problem behaviors. Their attitude about foster parenting changes. They don't hesitate to correct their foster child's misbehavior and teach a better way to behave. This doesn't make foster parenting any less challenging, but Foster Parents are able to see constructive results. They take the opportunity to teach whenever possible, and they use *Corrective Teaching* comfortably and confidently. *Corrective Teaching* will work for you, too, when used consistently with appropriate consequences.

# CHAPTER 16

# Teaching Self-Control

*"You're an idiot. I can't stand you!"*

*"Get outta my face, you jerk!"*

*"No way! I ain't gonna do that, and you can't make me!"*

One of the more frustrating aspects of being a Foster Parent is dealing with an angry, defiant foster child who simply refuses to do what you ask or escalates his or her negative behavior. The child may be yelling, hitting, arguing, throwing objects, or threatening you. This type of behavior can make you feel powerless, emotionally drained, or just plain furious.

If you have ever felt like this, you're not alone. Many Foster Parents face these situations. One thing is certain, however: Foster children must learn that negative, aggressive behavior is not acceptable and that it can be harmful to them and others. The sooner foster children learn to control their actions, the more success they'll have with stopping negative behavior. When children do not respond to *Corrective Teaching* and continue to misbehave or refuse to cooperate, it's time to use a process called *Teaching Self-Control.*

## What Is Teaching Self-Control?

There are three key parts to *Teaching Self-Control:*

1. Helping your foster child calm down.

2. Using *Corrective Teaching.*

3. Doing *Follow-Up Teaching.*

Each part will be explained in detail, but let's first take a brief look at what often happens when a foster child loses self-control and confronts a Foster Parent with angry, resistant, or aggressive behaviors.

For example, let's say a child has refused to follow an instruction and has started yelling at the Foster Parent. In these situations, a foster child is certainly not interested in, and in some cases not capable of, discussing the situation rationally. Generally, a great deal of talking by the Foster Parent does little to improve the situation. Often, the more the Foster Parent talks, the louder the child yells. The more the foster child yells, the louder the Foster Parent talks, and eventually the Foster Parent is yelling, too. This continues until one of the two decides that the argument is too painful and drops out. It can be the Foster Parent, who walks out of the room in disgust and anger, or it can be the foster child, who stomps off to the bedroom and slams the door. In either case, the problem has gotten worse, not better.

If you've had to deal with a situation like this with a child, you know how helpless you can feel. *Teaching Self-Control* gives Foster Parents a way to respond that can help resolve these situations in an orderly manner.

We all get angry at times, but when anger is vented through aggressive behavior, it becomes harmful to everyone involved. You want to teach your foster children self-control and self-discipline so they can identify how they're feeling and learn how to deal with these emotions in ways that won't lead to aggressive or harmful behavior. The goal of *Teaching Self-Control* is to help your foster children learn *self-control,* which involves teaching them how to control their behavior when they get upset.

> **Foster children must learn that negative, aggressive behavior is not acceptable.**

The first part of this teaching method is geared toward helping the Foster Parent and the foster child become calm. This way, both can work to resolve the problem rationally, without yelling and shouting. Very little can be accomplished if anger takes the place of logic.

The second part of *Teaching Self-Control* gives the Foster Parent an opportunity to teach the foster child some acceptable ways of behaving – some options to choose from – when he or she is upset. Like the other teaching methods you have learned, *Teaching Self-Control* emphasizes giving clear, specific descriptions of the child's behaviors, using consequences, and teaching the desired behavior.

The third part of *Teaching Self-Control* helps to prevent future problems by having the child practice skills later when the situation has cooled down. This is done to reinforce the teaching you and your child did earlier.

## How Teaching Self-Control Works

Each part of *Teaching Self-Control* is made up of smaller steps that are designed to calm the foster child and get him or her to respond to your teaching. Let's look at the steps first; an explanation of each one follows.

### Part 1: Calming Down

- Describe the problem behavior.

- Give clear instructions.

- Allow time to calm down.

### Part 2: Corrective Teaching

- Describe what your foster child could do differently next time.

- Give a reason.

- Practice what your foster child can do next time.

- Give a consequence.

### Part 3: Follow-Up Teaching

- Do Proactive Teaching later in the day to ensure that the original issue has been addressed.

- Teach and practice skills the child can use to prevent future "blow-ups."

# Part 1: Calming Down

### Describe the problem behavior.

Tell your foster child exactly what he or she is doing wrong. It's important to do this briefly. Your foster child may not be interested in listening to what you have to say at this time, so saying a lot won't help. You will have time to describe the problem in detail once your foster child settles down. Remember to be clear and specific with what you say. You should talk in a calm, level voice. Don't speak rapidly or try to say too much. For example, saying, *"Marcus, you're yelling at me and pacing around the room,"* gives the foster child a clear message about what he is doing.

At times, untrained Foster Parents say judgmental things when they dislike their foster child's behavior. *"Quit acting like a baby"* and *"You have a lousy attitude"* are two examples. Remember that these are perceptions and do not describe specific behaviors. Make sure that you simply and quickly describe what your foster child is doing wrong without becoming angry or accusatory. Say as little as possible while still getting your point across. **A good rule is to describe the behavior in 10 words or less.**

It also is helpful to use empathy. As discussed earlier, empathy means showing that you understand the other person's feelings. For instance, you might tell a child, *"I know you are upset right now. And I know what happened made you unhappy."* This starts the teaching sequence positively and shows your foster child that you care. It also helps you focus on your foster child's behavior rather than your own emotions.

## Give clear instructions.

Your purpose here is to help your foster child regain self-control, and utilize the staying calm strategies you and your foster child have developed during a neutral time. Tell the child exactly what you want him or her to do. Simple instructions, such as *"Please come over here and sit down"* or *"Please stop yelling at me,"* clearly state what your foster child needs to do. Don't give too many instructions or repeat them constantly; this might come across as lecturing or badgering. Simple, clear, calm instructions keep the focus on having your foster child regain self-control.

You also can continue to give instructions, such as *"Take a few deep breaths, and try to settle down"* or *"I'd like you to go to your room until you feel you can talk more calmly about your feelings."* Again, be brief, and remember to stay calm. By doing so, you will be setting a good example for your foster child. Showing you are calm and in control is likely to help him or her calm down, too.

**It is very important for you to practice these first two steps (describing the problem behavior and giving clear instructions).** The emphasis is on using clear messages to help calm your foster child. In addition to giving your foster child important information about his or her behavior, clear messages help keep you on track.

One more way to help to get certain situations under control is called the "five-second rule." This rule requires that other children leave the area and go to a predesignated area within five seconds. (Note: Use *Proactive Teaching* to let other children know what to do and where to go when the five-second rule is in effect. This preteaching can eliminate additional problems that the incident may trigger.) When the foster child is so upset that he or she may pose a threat to himself or herself or others or is likely to "blow up" quickly, tell any other children who are around that the five-second rule is in effect. This keeps other children safe and allows you to give the foster child your complete attention. It also helps the child calm down because he or she doesn't have an "audience" and therefore doesn't feel like he or she will "lose face" by backing down in front of the other children.

## Allow time to calm down.

Foster Parents tell us that this is the most important step in the process. If they remain calm, it's more likely that their foster child will calm down faster. Foster Parents also tell us that remembering this step has helped them focus on their foster child's behavior. Simply saying, *"We both need a little time to calm down. I'll be back in a few minutes,"* can be very effective. Remember: Sometimes, giving your foster child a little "space" helps him or her "save face." (Note: Continue to monitor children during this time, especially if you are concerned that they may harm themselves or others.) This additional time gives your foster child the opportunity to decide to use his or her staying calm plan. It also is a time when the child can decide to continue misbehaving or calm down. The focus of teaching during this step should be on staying calm and not the original issue.

As you take time to calm down, think of which skill you are going to teach next. Come back to the child as often as necessary. Ask questions, such as *"Are you ready to start following instructions?"* or *"Are you calmed down enough to talk to me?"*

Move to the second part of *Teaching Self-Control* when your foster child is able to answer you in a reasonably calm voice and pay attention to what you say. You're not going to have the happiest foster child at this point, but it's important that he or she can talk without losing self-control again.

Take your time. Give descriptions and instructions as needed. Most of all, be calm and in control of your emotions.

# Part 2: Corrective Teaching

## Describe what your foster child could do differently next time.

Give your foster child another way to express frustration or anger. Foster children have to learn that if they blow up when something doesn't go their way, it leads to more negative consequences. Foster Parents can rely on the *"Instead of…"* phrase. It goes like this: *"Instead of yelling and running out the door, just look at me, and say 'Okay'"; "Instead of cursing, try taking a deep breath and think of how to answer me"; "Instead of pacing the floor, why don't you sit on the couch?"*

The purpose of this phrase is to get foster children to think. The next time they're in a negative situation, if they just think about what happened, possibly something will click, and they will remember not to make the situation worse.

### Give a reason.

Give your foster child a reason why it's important for him or her to stay calm the next time. For example, you could say, *"If you use your self-control strategy when you're upset, it shows that you're trying to control your anger in a positive way. Then I'll be more likely to listen to what you want to tell me."*

The purpose of giving foster children a reason is to help them begin to see how changing their behavior can benefit them and/or others. Giving a reason every time increases the chances that they will behave appropriately in the future. This not only benefits them, but also makes your job as a Foster Parent easier.

### Practice what your foster child can do next time.

Now that your foster child knows what to do, it's important that he or she knows how to do it. By practicing, you are more likely to see the child use the behavior you want the next time he or she starts to get upset.

After the practice is over, let your foster child know what was done correctly and what needs improvement. **Be as positive as you can be and use lots of praise,** especially if your foster child is making a real effort to do what you ask.

## Give a consequence.

This is a crucial part of *Teaching Self-Control*. If there is a common mistake made by Foster Parents, it is that they forget to give a consequence. They get so wrapped up in stopping their foster child's negative behavior, or they are so pleased once all the yelling stops, that giving a consequence doesn't cross their minds. Others tell us that they just don't have the heart to give a consequence because they don't want to get the child more upset. But not providing a consequence for misbehavior means that the misbehavior is very likely to occur again. **Consequences help change behavior – don't be afraid to use them!**

There are several good reasons for waiting until the end of the teaching before your foster child earns a consequence. The child is calmer and more likely to accept the consequence. You also are calmer and more likely to deliver a fair consequence. It is human to let our emotions of anger or frustration influence our decisions about consequences. It is easy to overreact and give too severe a punishment. When you are both calm, delivering a consequence is much more likely to have the desired result – changing negative behavior.

# Part 3: Follow-Up Teaching

## Do Proactive Teaching later in the day to ensure that the original issue has been addressed.

After the consequence has been given and your foster child has calmed down, there is still some unfinished business. You and your child still need to work on the original issue that caused him or her to lose self-control. You can do this by using *Proactive Teaching* and practice later in the day when the child is completely calmed down. (Remember that the amount of time will vary from child to child.) It's easy to forget this step. It's quite likely that you'll be tired and won't want to chance another blow-up. Possibly, you'll just want to get this behind you and get on with the rest of your day. However, if you fail to address and attend to the original issue with more practice, the message your foster child gets is: *"I can lose control, and my foster parents won't deal with the original problem."*

## Teach and practice skills the child can use to prevent future blow-ups.

*Follow-Up Teaching* also is the time to teach and practice other skills that may help prevent future blow-ups in your foster home, in school, or in other settings (*Accepting "No" Answers, Following Instructions, Accepting Criticism,* etc.)

# Using Teaching Self-Control

Let's take a look at an example of using *Teaching Self-Control*. Here's the situation: A foster mom has just told her 10-year-old foster son, Shawn, that he can't go over to his friend's house because he hasn't finished cleaning his room. He yells, *"You idiot! I hate you! You never let me do anything!"* Then he runs to his room screaming and cursing.

(Some of the steps of *Teaching Self-Control* are followed by helpful hints for using the step.)

## Part I: Calming Down

**Describe the problem behavior.**

- Clearly tell the foster child what he is doing wrong.

- Use empathy statements.

  *"I understand it's hard to hear 'No' when you really want to do something. But when I told you 'No,' you began yelling and swearing."*

**Give clear instructions.**

- Describe what the child should do.

- Give options for calming down.

- Focus on praising the child for making an effort to calm down and follow instructions.

  *"Instead of yelling, please use your staying calm strategy. You can sit here in your room or listen to music like we talked about."*

**Allow time to calm down.**

- Give everyone a chance to calm down.

- Decide what to teach next. (Before leaving the area, tell your child that you're giving him or her a chance to calm down. Come back and ask the child if he is willing to talk.)

- Check for cooperative behavior.

  *"I'm going to give you some time to calm down. I'll be back in a few minutes to see if you're ready to work through this."*

  When your foster child is following instructions and is willing to talk with you about the problem, move from *Calming Down* to *Corrective Teaching.*

## Part 2: Corrective Teaching

**Describe what your foster child could do differently next time.**

- Think of a better way your foster child can react when he gets upset.

  *"Shawn, let's look at what you can do the next time you get upset. A better choice the next time you think you're getting mad is to use your staying calm plan and ask me if you can go to your room and calm down."*

**Give a reason.**

- Relate it to the foster child.

  *"If you learn to calm yourself down without yelling and cursing, we can get the problem solved*

*faster and you won't lose any, or certainly not as many, of your privileges."*

**Practice what your foster child can do next time.**

- Practicing will make it more likely that your foster child will do what is expected.

Foster mom: *"Let's give this a try. When you ask me if you can go out and play, and you start to get really angry, what should you do?"*

Shawn: *"Ask if I can go to my room to chill for a while."*

Foster mom: *"Great! Okay. And what are you going to do in your room to calm down?"*

Shawn: *"Listen to music or draw."*

- Let him know how he practiced.

    *"Very good. You asked me if you could go to your room. And you asked me in a nice voice tone. Excellent!"*

**Give a consequence.**

- This will help prevent the problem from occurring again.

    *"For yelling and swearing and not using your staying calm plan, you will not be able to go to your friend's house for two days. Please go wash your hands for dinner. If you want to earn back some of the time at your friend's house, we could practice how to stay calm some more after the dishes are done."*

## Part 3: Follow-Up Teaching

**Do *Proactive Teaching* later in the day to ensure that the original issue has been addressed.**

Foster mom: *"Shawn, earlier in the day you became angry after I told you 'No' when you asked to go to a friend's house. Can you tell me how you accept a 'No' answer?"*

Shawn: *"Look at you; say 'Okay'; don't argue."*

Foster mom: *"Great! Let's go ahead and practice Accepting 'No' Answers."*

**Teach and practice skills the child can use to prevent future blow-ups.**

- Teaching specific skills helps foster children know what is expected of them. Once you have addressed the original issue, here are some skills that Foster Parents frequently find helpful to teach during Follow-Up Teaching:

  *Asking for Help*

  *Accepting Criticism*

  *Accepting "No" Answers*

  *Following Instructions*

  *Disagreeing with Others*

  *Appropriately Expressing Feelings (anger, sadness, disappointment, etc.)*

  *Apologizing*

Remember: This is an example. In real-life situations, your foster child probably won't cooperate this quickly. He or she may go from being uncooperative to being calm and then suddenly to being uncooperative again. Some foster children have a lot of stamina when they're upset. You may also have to deal with other distractions in these situations: Your other children need something; the phone rings; the soup is boiling over on the stove, and others. Interactions with your foster child do not occur in a vacuum. In these instances, use the skills you learned in the chapter, "Staying Calm," and adapt the teaching steps and your teaching style to the situation. Stick to simple descriptions and instructions, continue to use empathy, and stay calm.

## Teaching Self-Control to Toddlers

For Foster Parents of children who are younger (ages 2 to 5), we recommend a slightly different approach to using *Teaching Self-Control.* While it uses some of the same basic steps we just discussed, this approach involves fewer parts, fewer steps, and briefer instructions. That's because toddlers and preschoolers have a much shorter attention span than older kids.

*Teaching Self-Control* for younger children has two parts: *Calming Down* and *Follow-Up Teaching.*

In this version of *Teaching Self-Control, Calming Down* consists of these steps:

1. Describe the problem behavior.

2. Give clear instructions.

3. Allow time to calm down.

4. Check for cooperation.

Here is an example of how the *Calming Down* part might sound:

Situation: A 4-year-old screams and throws toys when told it's time for bed.

**1. Describe the problem behavior.**

- Show and tell what your child is doing that is not calm behavior.

  *"I'm sorry you don't want to go to bed. But right now you are screaming and throwing toys."*

- Stay calm.

- Be understanding.

**2. Give clear instructions.**

- Show and tell your child how to calm down.

  *"Please stop. Why don't you try counting to five to calm down?"*

- Be brief.

**3. Allow time to calm down.**

- Tell your child to go to a safe place or take your child to a safe place.

  *"I'm going to give you a few minutes to work on calming yourself down. Please go sit on the couch and I'll check on you later."*

- Or remove yourself once your child is safe.

### 3. Check for cooperation.

- See if your child is ready to cooperate by giving simple instructions.

  *"Are you ready to listen now?* (Child nods head.) *Okay. Why don't you come sit down beside me so we can talk."*

*Follow-Up Teaching* involves using one of the following options, with each option providing a consequence for the child's behavior. (To choose an option, decide what your primary goal is and what you want your child to learn from this situation. You should base your teaching on your child's age and developmental level, how severe the out-of-control behavior was, and what was going on before the out-of-control behavior occurred.):

- **Redirect** – Involve your child in another constructive activity.

- **Redo/Overlearn** – Have your child appropriately repeat an action or statement he or she did incorrectly.

- **Undo** – Reverse or correct the effects of a negative behavior.

- **Use time-out** – Remove your child from fun things for a short, quiet period.

- **Practice calming skills** – Rehearse taking a deep breath or counting to 10 when your child begins to get upset.

- **Practice social skills** – Teach a behavior that could help the child avoid getting frustrated or angry and prevent the problem behavior from occurring.

- **Give additional consequence** – Remove a privilege or possession for a short period of time.
- **Return to the original issue** – Ask your child what happened to cause the outburst and together find ways to correct it in the future.

Don't be surprised if you use more than one skill or tool at a time to help your children improve their behavior. It's sometimes easy to "piggyback" these options because they can be completed in a short time.

Foster Parents of one child might choose different options than Foster Parents of another child, even when the children did the same thing. It all depends on what the Foster Parents believe their child needs to learn most. Let's look at an example: A boy bites another child during an argument over a toy they both want. One Foster Parent might choose to immediately put the boy in time-out, firmly say, *"Don't bite. It hurts people,"* and then give his attention to the other child. Another Foster Parent might want to teach the boy the skill of apologizing by having him tell the other child he is sorry and then offering to do something nice to make up for biting. Another Foster Parent might remove a possession or activity from the boy, such as taking away the toy that originally caused the conflict and putting *it* in time-out. And another Foster Parent might concentrate on helping the boy practice calming-down strategies.

With younger children, a Foster Parent's tolerances and point of view play a big part in how he or she uses *Follow-Up Teaching*. In each of the responses to the biting situation, the Foster Parents chose methods they thought would work best to teach their kids self-control.

Other skills you have learned in this book also can be used in *Follow-Up Teaching* with younger children.

**Effective Praise** works well in situations where children calm down before their behavior gets worse or when they have shown improvement in their ability to calm down on their own. Foster Parents may praise children for taking time to calm down, for calming down more quickly than in the past, or even for apologizing for things they said or did. It may sound like this: *"Good job! You remembered to take a deep breath and you calmly said, 'I'm mad,' all by yourself. See how easy that was. Now why don't you tell me what's bothering you."*

**Proactive Teaching** is helpful when Foster Parents feel that additional teaching and practicing is needed. Foster Parents can use *Proactive Teaching* to teach a new calming-down strategy or a social skill that may have helped the child in the original situation. *Proactive Teaching* is probably most appropriate when a child's emotional behaviors need attention, but are not overly aggressive or inappropriate.

For example: *"The next time you feel angry, say, 'I'm mad.' Then maybe I can help you find a better way to handle it. Let's talk about some ways you can keep from getting so upset next time."*

**Corrective Teaching** can also be used during *Follow-Up Teaching*. *Corrective Teaching* is most appropriate when a child's initial problem behaviors are so disruptive that they must be addressed, or when a Foster Parent recognizes that a child uses emotional outbursts to avoid consequences. In situations like this, a negative consequence becomes necessary to show a child that frequent and severe behaviors only make things worse.

This teaching might sound like this: *"I'm glad you are feeling calmer now. Earlier, you would not stop yelling or go to your room to calm down when I asked. Since you didn't, you will have to sit in time-out for five minutes."* After time-out is over, the Foster Parent says, *"Thanks for sitting so quietly in time-out. Now let's practice what you can do the next time you feel upset."*

## Why Teach Self-Control?

Think about this for a minute: If your 4-year-old foster son throws himself on the floor and kicks and screams to get his way every time he gets frustrated or upset with someone or something, how do you think he will try to get what he wants next time? Right. He will throw a tantrum.

If your 8-year-old foster daughter argues and whines until you give in, what do you think will happen the next time she wants something? Exactly. She will argue and whine. If your teenage foster son yells and threatens you when you tell him he can't go out with his friends, and he eventually gets to go anyway, what do you think will happen the next time you tell him he can't go out? Yes. Yelling and threatening.

So when asking, "Why teach self-control?", the answer is clear. You want your foster child to be able to respond to frustrating situations in healthy, not harmful, ways. Maintaining self-control helps children get along with family members, do better in school, develop friendships, keep jobs, and take advantage of opportunities that would otherwise be lost.

## When to Use Teaching Self-Control

Foster Parents report that they use *Teaching Self-Control* in three main types of situations:

- **When a foster child comes in to a home with a history of angry outbursts or physical aggression.** Foster Parents can use *Proactive Teaching* to teach a child self-control *before* he or she becomes uncooperative.

- **When a foster child misbehaves and will not respond to *Corrective Teaching*.** Instead, the foster child continues the misbehavior or the misbehavior worsens.

- **When a foster child blows up** – a sudden and intense emotional outburst during which the foster child refuses to do anything the Foster Parents ask.

Most often, good use of social skills by foster children helps them deal with stressful situations in constructive ways.

# Helpful Hints

### Stay calm.

Staying calm is much easier when you stay on task. Implement all of the steps of *Teaching Self-Control;* concentrating on your foster child's behavior is much easier when you have a framework to follow. *Teaching Self-Control* gives you a set of effective steps for responding to your foster children when you need it most. Those are the times when you are the most frustrated, upset, or exasperated. Your foster children may argue with what you say or call you names. They may say you don't care about them or tell you how unfair you are. They may say things to make you feel guilty or angry or useless. If you get caught up in these side issues, you lose sight of your original purpose – to teach your foster child self-control. You can lose sight of the original problem and how you need to deal with it. If you find yourself responding to what your foster child is saying, remember to use a key phrase like, *"We'll talk about that when you calm down."* Staying on task can keep you from arguing or losing your temper.

### Seek help.

As we previously mentioned, your foster child sometimes will not respond to your teaching right away. He or she may continue to be uncooperative by yelling, screaming, being aggressive, or simply ignoring you and not following instructions. These situations can be frustrating and tiring. If you get frustrated, talk with someone from your agency about how to better handle the situation. Sometimes, it's easier for a person who is not directly involved in the situation to clearly see a possible solution or provide you with helpful suggestions on how to better handle the situation.

**Watch your physical actions.**

Throughout the process, be aware of your physical actions. Some Foster Parents find that sitting down helps them calm the situation more quickly. When adults – particularly fathers – stand up, they tend to appear more threatening. This only makes matters worse and makes it less likely that the foster child will calm down.

Pointing your finger, putting your hands on your hips, scowling, leaning over your foster child, and raising a fist all are examples of physical actions that tend to increase tension in these emotionally charged situations. Try to avoid these gestures. Keep your hands in your pockets, cross them over your chest, or find something to do with them other than waving them at your foster child.

It is also important to pay attention to how close you are to your foster child. To ensure your safety and to avoid any physical aggression, it's important that you stay a safe distance away. Be aware of your surroundings, and don't allow yourself to get backed into a corner, caught on the stairs, or blocked in a doorway. Remember that your foster child may not be fully in control of his or her emotions at times and therefore is unpredictable. The safety of every-

one present is most important. Any teaching or consequences can wait until your foster child has had a chance
to cool down.

### Plan ahead for consequences.

It helps to have consequences set up in advance; for
example, you could tell your foster daughter, *"Sarah,
when I tell you 'No,' sometimes you want to argue with me.
Then you get mad and start yelling. From now on, if you
do that, you will lose your phone privileges."* Then explain
to Sarah why she needs to accept a "No" answer and why
she shouldn't argue or yell. Planned consequences are consistent; if Sarah loses self-control, she is aware of the negative consequence she will receive. Also, planned consequences help you avoid giving unreasonable or harsh consequences that stem from your anger.

### Let children earn back lost consequences.

Remember that letting children earn back some of their
lost privileges helps to keep them motivated to learn and
practice new skills. Children should be able to earn back
up to half of the privileges that are taken away.

### Follow through on side issues.

As your foster child calms down and you complete the
teaching sequence, numerous side issues can arise. For
example, some situations may call for a problem-solving
approach. Your foster child may not have the knowledge or
experience to deal with a certain situation. Take time to
help find solutions. Other situations may call for a firm,

matter-of-fact ending to *Teaching Self-Control:* *"Okay, we've practiced what to do. Now go to Jeremy's room and pleasantly apologize to him."*

Still other situations may call for an empathetic, understanding approach. Some foster children cry after an intense situation. They just don't know how to handle what they're feeling. In such situations, you could say, *"Let's sit down and talk about what's been going on to make you feel so angry. Maybe I can help. At least, I can listen."* Take the opportunity to help your foster child by using whatever you believe is the best approach. Sometimes, going through the rough times together forms the tightest emotional bonds.

## Summary

Foster Parents must have a bountiful supply of patience if their foster children have a problem with self-control. The wisest Foster Parents are those who realize that learning self-control is an ongoing process. They are skeptical – as you should be – of anyone who claims that self-control can be taught immediately. They know it takes a long time. Don't try to rush the learning process; expecting too much too soon can create more problems than it solves. Be attentive to small accomplishments, and praise even the smallest bit of progress your foster child makes. While you're at it, give yourself a big pat on the back. *Teaching Self-Control* is a tough job, and you wouldn't do it if you weren't committed to helping your foster child.

As you teach self-control, look for positive changes. Your foster child may have fewer angry outbursts, the outbursts won't last as long, or they won't be nearly as serious as they were. *Teaching Self-Control* helps Foster Parents and foster children break the painful argument cycle. When tension is greatest in the family, *Teaching Self-Control* gives everyone a constructive way to get problems resolved.

# CHAPTER 17

# Solving Problems and Making Decisions

Children and adolescents frequently must make decisions on the spur of the moment. Often, they make poor decisions because they lack life experiences. Other times, kids tend to look at solutions to problems as black and white; either you do something or you don't. And many of our foster children make decisions based on whatever emotion they are feeling at the time. Seldom do kids think ahead about how a decision could affect them later.

All of us make decisions every day. Some are simple, such as what to eat for lunch or what TV program to watch. Others are more important and harder to figure out, such as whom to trust or what to do with our careers. Usually we're able to weigh all of the options we have and make an intelligent decision. We're able to identify what is important and what is minor and make our decisions accordingly. We have had enough experience solving problems to logically figure out what to do. But to children and adolescents, especially those who have had trouble at home and been sent to other placements, every problem can seem like an insurmountable obstacle. It is our job to give our kids the skills and experience they need to overcome the problems in their lives and learn how to make good decisions that will benefit them in the future.

Children will have to decide how to spend their allowances, who to hang around with, or how to respond to the unique challenges of being a foster child. Look at some examples of foster kids who made poor decisions: A teacher criticized Jon's homework so he dropped the class. A girl Sara knows made fun of her, so Sara trashed the girl's locker at school. Someone asked Sean to a party where there was alcohol; he knew he would get in trouble but didn't want to be left out, so he went and the party was raided. In each of these situations, there were many wiser options, but these kids didn't have the skills to choose them.

There is a simple method that you can teach your foster kids that will help them make better decisions. It doesn't take a great deal of time, and it works. This problem-solving method is called *P-O-P*. The letters stand for **Problem, Options,** and **Plan.** Let's look at each step.

## Identify the Problem

Before you can solve anything, you have to know exactly what the problem is. This may sound elementary, but people often rush into making a decision before they've properly identified the whole problem. Sometimes, they get caught up in their feelings rather than using logic. We all can make a "mountain out of a mole-hill" when we're upset or pressured.

Teach your foster kids to put their emotions on a shelf before they attempt to solve a problem. That will help them look at a situation logically. (Help your foster kids learn the same techniques presented in Chapter 14, "Staying Calm.") That's tough for anyone of us to do, and it may be especially difficult for younger children and adolescents. But before good decisions can be made, kids have to learn how to stay calm so they don't make a decision based on anger, frustration, or excitement.

**To children and adolescents, every problem can seem like an insurmountable obstacle.**

Kids also must know how to ask themselves questions that will help them piece together the whole problem, not just the obvious parts of it. Tell them to be like a newspaper reporter who always asks "who," "what," "when," and "where." Ask them specific, open-ended questions that encourage discussion and dialogue. Avoid asking questions that a child can answer with one-word responses such as "Yes," "No," "Fine," or "Good." Instead, ask questions such as *"What did you do then?"* or *"What happened after you said that?"* Questions like these allow kids to sort through their feelings and get a better picture of the whole situation. With younger children or developmentally disadvantaged kids, you might have to ask numerous questions to help the child understand the situation. It's also a good idea to summarize the information in a specific, easy-to-understand manner. Ask your foster child if your summary is correct before continuing.

## List and Consider the Options

Once you and your foster child have identified the problem, talk about different ways to solve it. Teach children to ask themselves questions such as *"What would happen if I did this?"* and to think about what could happen if they choose a certain option. This is a great time for kids to be active in learning how to solve problems by themselves and to think things through. Your role is that of coach and advisor. Don't rush to provide options or solutions, even though they may seem obvious to you. Because you care about the well-being of your kids, it's natural to want to "save" them by solving all of their problems. You must realize, however, that you won't always be there to help them, so the most important thing you can do is teach them to make decisions on their own.

Helping your foster child come up with options is a great way to help kids understand that there are many ways to handle a problem. It teaches them patience and logic and actually gives them hope because they are discovering that they do have some control over their lives. Too many times, kids think that there isn't anything they can do that will work out; they let adults make all the decisions or just let things happen. Coming up with their own options shows them that they can do many things that can make a difference and possibly even work out for them.

Kids often will want to choose the first option that comes to mind, or they may see only one solution and not explore any others. They may think that the situation is hopeless and just want to give up. Teach them to be patient and think things through so that they can find several different ways to solve a problem. This may mean asking frequent questions to get them to think through all the choices they have. Say things like, *"Try to think of something else you could do"* or *"What else could solve the problem?"* You may need to consistently ask these questions until kids eventually learn how to make decisions without your guidance, especially as children are first learning the *P-O-P* method.

Many circumstances can affect the outcomes of each option. How well an option works depends upon the situation, how well the young person carries out what was decided, and the reactions of other people involved. That's why it's important to stress to your foster kids that there are no guarantees that an option will work. They are making a decision based on all **Don't rush to provide options or solutions, even though they may seem obvious to you.** the information they have at hand. While they may believe they're doing what's best, they don't always have complete control over the outcome.

Have your foster kids tell you what might go wrong with an option, taking into account the situation or the person with whom they're dealing. Then have them tell you what could go right. Do the positives outweigh the negatives? Sometimes, an option isn't perfect, but it may be the best one available. Also, kids need to realize that some negative things might happen, but that the decision they make is the best one in the long run. Usually, you should limit the options to four; any more than that tends to be confusing. Again, for younger children or those just learning the process, you may have to suggest some workable options. Two might be all they are able to consider, so keep the number of options at a minimum until they become better at doing it on their own.

## Make a Plan

After your foster child has chosen an option, have him or her make a plan to put the option to work. The first two steps involved thinking; this step involves doing. If the plan requires having your foster child talk with someone, it's a very good idea to practice what the child is going to say and do. If the plan involves completing a series of steps, figure out a workable method and time frame before you have your foster child take action.

The *P-O-P* method can be used with children of different ages. The process is exactly the same. Of course, with adolescents, problems can become very complex. With younger kids, helping them come up with options is usually the hardest part.

## How P-O-P Works

Here's an example where a foster mother is helping her 10-year-old foster son solve a problem with some other kids at school.

### Identify the problem.

Sara noticed that her foster son, Reggie, came home from school looking puzzled. She goes to his room to talk to him.

Sara: *"What's going on Reggie? You look a little down about something."*

Reggie: *"Some of the guys at school are asking me questions about why I'm in foster care."*

Sara: *"And that bothers you?"*

Reggie: *"Well yeah. I just don't know what to tell them."*

Sara: *"That can be tough. Sometimes we don't know how other people are going to react if we tell them something personal. Can you describe exactly how it makes you feel when they ask you questions?"*

Reggie: *"Well, mostly I feel like I'm different from everyone else."*

Sara: *"Okay, so the problem is how to answer the kids when they ask you these questions. Right?"*

Reggie: *"Yeah."*

## List the options.

Sara: *"Okay, what are some ways you could answer their questions?"*

Reggie: *"I could tell them to bug off. That it's none of their business."*

Sara: *"Yes you could. What might happen if you did that?"*

Reggie: *"I dunno. Some guys might get mad and think I'm stuck up or not want to hang around with me anymore."*

Sara: *"Would they stop asking you questions?"*

Reggie: *"They might, but they'd probably start making fun of me."*

Sara: *"And you don't want that, do you?"*

Reggie: *"No way. I'd like to have some friends to play with."*

Sara: *"Okay, what's something else you could do?"*

Reggie: *"I could tell them everything about my family and why I'm really here and not with my family."*

Sara: *"How would you feel about doing that?"*

Reggie: *"Then I'd really be worried that they'd think I was some kind of freak or something. Or they might make fun of my family."*

Sara: *"That might happen. I take it you don't think that's a good thing to do?"*

Reggie: *"No. I'd feel bad if I told everyone about what's happened at home."*

Sara: *"Well, so far you've mentioned two things that were really far apart – telling the guys nothing or telling them everything. Is there another way to handle it without doing either of these things?"*

Reggie: *"I dunno."*

Sara: *"Well, let's see. Maybe there's something you could do that is kind of in between. What about just coming up with a couple of lines to say to anyone who asks you. Something like, 'Yeah, my family's having problems right now, and I'm in a foster home until things get better.' Do you think that would help get the guys off your back?"*

Reggie: *"Yeah, it might. At least I'm telling them something. Maybe they'd just leave it alone after that."*

Sara: *"Do you want to try that?"*

Reggie: *"Okay."*

## Make a plan.

Sara: *"Okay, that sounds good. Let's practice. I'll ask you some questions and you say, 'Yeah. my family's having some problems right now and I'm staying in a foster home until things get better."*

271

Reggie: *"Okay."*

> Sara then practices with Reggie by asking ques-
> tions in a variety of voice tones and responding
> in a different way each time Reggie replies.
> Then they come up with a back-up plan in case
> the kids don't stop asking questions. Sara also
> reviews each of the problem-solving steps with
> Reggie. On a piece of paper, she writes down
> *P-O-P* in big letters and what each letter stands
> for, then tells Reggie to remember to use *P-O-P*
> whenever other problems come up.

Sara: *"Great job of coming up with some ways to
handle the problem Reggie. You really thought
this whole thing out. Thanks for telling me
about it, too. I always want to know when
things are bothering you."*

Regardless of how old your foster kids are, *P-O-P* gives them a practical way to solve problems. It stops them from making hasty decisions and helps them arrive at workable solutions. Simply remembering the name *P-O-P* helps kids stop and think before reacting.

It's a good idea to practice using the *P-O-P* method when there isn't an immediate problem; it helps kids get comfortable with this problem-solving skill. For example, you could make up a story about another kid who had a problem and ask your foster child how he or she would handle it. Or, you could look ahead to future events or situations you know your foster child will face and use the

*P-O-P* method to prepare your child for them. The more times your foster child practices using the skill, the better equipped he or she will be to handle routine problems.

*P-O-P* also can be used for setting short- and long-term goals or making plans. Many small problems crop up every day, and *P-O-P* is an excellent way for kids to come up with solutions. They can plan how to use their allowance, how to plan their free time, or possibly how to make the situation in their family better.

Of course, any time you help kids make a decision, there's a risk that something can go wrong. No one can be 100 percent positive that things will work out exactly as planned. An unexpected event or another person can throw everything off. Or another problem can come up that is more serious and needs immediate attention. Let your foster kids know that sometimes things won't work out as planned. Then go back and figure out why the plan didn't work.

## Additional Suggestions

**Don't use P-O-P to settle moral or legal issues.**

Occasionally, children face situations that are illegal or immoral or that will harm them or others. The responses to these situations should be automatic. When foster children first arrive in your home, you should set rules and guidelines that they should follow. And, as mentioned earlier, there are some situations where your foster child won't have complete control over making a decision. You have certain obligations concerning your foster child's placement, and that may mean not allowing your foster child to make certain decisions or solve certain problems. However, when

**P-O-P also can be used for setting short- and long-term goals or making plans.**

there is something he or she can do to make the outcome a little bit better, that should be the focus of using *P-O-P.* Possibly, your foster child can see that he or she can think through a troubling situation without feeling overwhelmed or making the situation worse.

**Use P-O-P to reconsider bad decisions.**

Sometimes, foster children may choose options that are not good for them. In these cases, clearly state your disapproval, repeat the problems that those options could cause, and let your foster child know the consequences of making that choice. For example, if your 14-year-old foster daughter decides to fight another girl who has been bullying her, let her know that you don't want her to fight and why. You can explain the consequences she will earn if she decides to fight and how they may affect her. Sometimes, despite all of your efforts, children make bad decisions. When that occurs, rely on all of the other teaching techniques you have learned in this book. If possible, help your foster child go back through the *P-O-P* method to find another solution to the problem.

**Offer your support.**

While you want to encourage your foster children to make decisions on their own, you need to let them know that you will be there to help at all times. Support their attempts at implementing a plan, and provide guidance and empathy when needed. If a plan doesn't work out as expected, return to the *P-O-P* format and try again.

**Practice the plan.**

Help your foster child practice putting the plan into effect. Practice might involve role-playing the situation so that your foster child can try out the words or actions needed to carry out the plan. Practice helps the child feel confident and comfortable about the plan and greatly increases the chances for success.

**Follow up with your foster child.**

Ask if the plan worked, ask questions about what was said or done, and ask if he or she was satisfied with the outcome. This is an excellent time to praise your foster child for trying to solve a problem, even if the plan didn't work as well as expected.

## Summary

This chapter has looked at just a few of the many possible situations where children and adolescents can use the *P-O-P* problem-solving process. *P-O-P* is practical and can be applied in many different situations. Most importantly, it is an effective way for you to give your foster children the confidence and skills needed to solve problems and to think on their own.

# CHAPTER 18

# Creating a Strong Spiritual Foundation

### *by Val J. Peter*

This chapter is a brief introduction to how spirituality can be an effective element in caring for children. Many child-care programs pay only lip service to the healing power of religion in a child's or family's life. We at Girls and Boys Town know from experience that without solid spiritual underpinnings, our children will be swept out with the tide of alienation, despair, and bitterness that has come into their lives.

On the other hand, there are programs that make religion the total explanation for everything. We at Girls and Boys Town know from experience that children will not get better unless they learn skills, build relationships, and develop self-discipline. No matter how much religion may help, if these three elements are missing, the program normally won't work. Faith, hope, and love alone are not enough. That's why we have found a middle ground between these two extremes.

## Helping the Child Become Whole

When children come into foster homes, they might have experienced abandonment, neglect, physical abuse, psychological abuse, spiritual abuse, sexual abuse, and many other problems. All the helping techniques described in this book, important as they are, tend to make changes in the exterior behavior of boys and girls. But we know from long years of experience that without a spiritual foundation, these external changes simply will not last in a vast majority of children. Children will not make the new behaviors they learn a permanent part of their lives.

Though a child may appear to make a great deal of progress during his or her first few weeks in a foster home, our work is only beginning. More often than not, in this short time, children have not let this experience yet touch their hearts. We know that it is only when a child experiences the miracle of healing in the heart that beauty, goodness, faith, hope, and love (God's gracious gifts) can be released. It is only then that we are able to complete the process of helping a child become whole again.

As a Foster Parent, you have the opportunity to help the children in your care learn that their lives will not make sense without a strong spiritual foundation. That foundation includes living a life of strong personal faith.

Each and every child comes from the hand of God. The good Lord puts us on this earth for a purpose. We are not random, isolated beings. The realization of our fundamental relationship with the Lord, who puts us here for a purpose, is enormously therapeutic for kids, especially for kids who are in out-of-home placements. A healthy relationship with the Lord is a missing link in the lives of so many kids who otherwise would see no purpose and no exit from all the troubles that have surrounded them.

Our founder, Father Flanagan, in his own day changed the way America thought of her abandoned and orphaned children. His convictions about the importance of religious formation for young people are summed up in his famous phrase, *"Every boy (and girl) must learn to pray. How he (and she) prays is up to him (and her)."* I know that today in America this is not considered politically correct. But it is true. And it is necessary. Why? Because kids can't get better without it. Let's go into some detail.

I know of many foster home programs, especially those run by the state, that offer a nondescript, uninspiring optional worship opportunity. The state gives

> **Without a spiritual foundation, external changes simply will not last.**

only lip service to religious needs. There are no prayers at meals. Kids are not encouraged to pray at bedtime. They are not encouraged to read their Scriptures. And they are simply not taught that if you are powerless before the negative forces in your life, then you desperately need to get in touch with a "Higher Power."

It is silly and naive to believe that we can build a moral society without belief in a Creator whose moral laws are to govern our lives. Basing moral norms on the majority opinion of society is perilous, indeed. It does not instill virtue in children, and without virtue, they cannot get better. And, of course, America will fail, too. A boy or girl who lies, cheats, steals, and acts out sexually will not get better. Father Flanagan was right: *"Every boy (and girl) must learn to pray."*

## Importance of Religion

Let me tell two stories that illustrate the importance of religion in the lives of foster children.

*Amy was 14 when she came into our program. Her problems were drug and alcohol use, sexual acting out, stealing, and truancy from school. We did not know until six months after she arrived at our doorstep that she had been repeatedly sexually abused by her father since she was in the third grade.*

*Then there is Jesse. He is 15 years old. His family moves a lot. He was in three psychiatric hospitals before arriving at Boys Town; he tried to take his life five times. His father is a raging alcoholic who has beaten Jesse ever since the boy was 3 years old.*

Amy and Jesse have four characteristics in common.

### Powerlessness

Amy feels powerless to stop the abuse that has been happening to her. Month after month, year after year, she was powerless before the advances of her father. In her mind, her father was all-powerful.

The first characteristic of Jesse is also a terrible, oppressive feeling of powerlessness because of the beatings his father gave him year after year. There was nothing he could do to stop it. In Jesse's eyes, his father was all-powerful.

Both Jesse and Amy describe their fathers as having all the power. Who is described as "all-powerful?" God. Amy's father and Jesse's father displaced God from these children's lives and made it impossible for them to get in touch with a Higher Power. No wonder they had lost hope; the all-powerful person in their lives was harmful and hurtful.

## Taking the Blame

The second characteristic Amy and Jesse share is that they blame themselves. Jesse says, *"It is my fault that my father beats me."* Why does he say that? Because when he was 3 years old and his father first beat him, he ran to his mother, who said: *"If you wouldn't make so much noise, your father wouldn't beat you."* That was repeated over and over, year after year. Whose fault was it? Jesse's. His father said so often: *"If you weren't such a disobedient and disrespectful kid, you wouldn't need this discipline."*

How can Amy possibly think it is her fault? It's easy to explain. Amy will tell you that she always liked some of the attention her father gave her. She didn't like the sexual part, but at first she liked being called "daddy's special girl" who had "special privileges" and got to do "special things." Her father repeatedly told her, *"I know you like it"* and *"If you hadn't started jumping on my lap with your little nightgown on when you were in the third grade, this would never have happened."*

Jesse's father says it's not his fault: *"You'd drink too if you had all the troubles I have."* And Amy's father says it's not his fault: *"Isn't it better she learns this from me than some stupid kid?"*

So both Amy and Jesse take the blame, and they feel powerless to stop it – even more reason to have no hope.

## Keeping a Secret

The third characteristic of Jesse and Amy is that what has happened to them is a secret. Amy's father told her: *"If you ever tell your mother, she won't believe it. Even if she does believe it, you'll be thrown out of the house."* Well, she told her mother, and her mother didn't believe her at first. And when her mother did believe her, guess who got sent out of the house? Her father? No. Amy did. The victim was punished.

How did Amy keep "the secret"? By getting into drugs, alcohol, stealing, and truancy. She was just known as "a wild kid." Who could have suspected how it all started?

How did Jesse keep his "secret"? Through prosocial behavior – doing well in school, always earning good grades, playing in the band, being well liked. Nobody would suspect that he was such a "bad" person that his father had to beat him. The only thing he would not do is play sports. Why? Because playing sports meant having to take off his clothes in the locker room, and people would see the black and blue marks. The problem with Jesse, of course, was that he could only stand it for so long, and then he tried to end his life. And when he did, people said: *"How could such a successful young man do that?"*

## Love

The fourth characteristic Amy and Jesse share may seem like a strange one. Amy loves her father, and in some strange way, her father loves her. She just wishes he would act like a father. And Jesse loves his father. He just wishes the beatings would stop and that his father would start going to Alcoholics Anonymous. And in some strange way, his father does love him.

Unless Jesse and Amy get in touch with a Higher Power, they will forever feel powerless, without hope, and filled with guilt. Religion isn't a luxury for Amy and Jesse. It's not a social nicety. It's an absolute necessity in their lives. Anyone who is familiar with Alcoholics Anonymous understands its first principle: *"I am powerless. I need to get in touch with the Higher Power."*

We have far too many kids like Jesse and Amy. Far, far too many.

## Inner Healing

Many children who come into foster care have suffered from abandonment and neglect, and other problems. All the technologies that we describe in this book, important as they are, will initially help change only the exterior behavior of our boys and girls.

After a few months in one of Girls and Boys Town's many programs, our boys and girls will begin to behave better on the surface. They will look like they have really made immense progress. But so far, up to that point, we have only touched the outside, the surface of things. It is only when children allow the Lord into their hearts and experience a miracle of inner healing and release in their lives that they know the goodness, the beauty, faith, hope, and love that are God's gracious gifts. It is only then that they make up their minds to use the skills we have taught them after they leave our program. That is why religion is a definite priority in all our programs for boys and girls. And that is why we respect and enhance the religious traditions of youth who come to us.

## Goals for Spiritual Development

Foster Parents bear the awesome responsibility of instilling sound spiritual and religious practices. At the same time, they must be careful not to inhibit the free exercise of conscience by foster children by forcing or trying to convince them to adopt a certain faith or set of religious beliefs.

At Girls and Boys Town today, we do not proselytize (i.e., force children to convert from one faith to another). So if a youth comes from a Methodist background, we will definitely try to make him or her a better Methodist. And if a youth is a Jew, we're going to try to make him or her a better Jew and help him or her go to synagogue weekly.

And if a youth is a follower of Islam, we're going to help him or her go to the Islamic Center every week.

It is important to understand why. It is not because we are indifferent. It is not because we think, "One religion is as good as another." It is because the children who come to us are a "captive population." They are prisoners of tragic circumstances. Their prison bars consist of abandonment, abuse, neglect, violence, and suicide. There are special ethical rules for captive populations. One of

> **Respect and enhance the religious traditions of youth who come to you.**

them is that caregivers should not proselytize. We have too much power, and they have too little freedom. For this reason, proselytism would violate the covenant of loyalty that we have with them.

We have very specific suggestions for helping you guide the youngsters in your care on their spiritual journey:

### Help youth find spiritual guidance.

Foster Parents can help children realize that they need to put their faith in a power beyond themselves. Foster Parents can help children appreciate and cherish their fundamental relationship with God, who loves and understands them.

In the past, foster children may have had either negative experiences with religion or almost no spiritual experiences at all. The difficulties that may have plagued their homes – alcoholism, a stressful divorce, domestic violence, abuse of every kind, suicide, abandonment – all have made God seem far away and indifferent to them. These children need to see warm images of God, and you need to provide those for them.

**Be a role model.**

Foster Parents can model faith through their behavior, their thoughts, and their feelings. Role models are respected and admired people who make the faith life attractive by encouraging others in gentle and joyful ways to witness to their faith. As role models, it is important that our attitude encourages the spiritual life in our homes and in our programs.

**Attend religious services.**

To be good role models, Foster Parents are strongly encouraged to attend religious services with their foster children and encourage participation in activities that promote spiritual growth. If a child is placed in a home that practices a faith that is different from his or her faith, Foster Parents are very much encouraged to attend services with that child in his or her church. By their attendance at religious services, Foster Parents can enhance the worship experience for their children and help them view the experience as an important family activity.

Most communities have a variety of activities that complement the development of a child's spiritual life. These activities – church youth groups, Bible study, Sunday school programs, and summer church camps – help youth find ways to strengthen their faith.

**Do community service or charity work with your foster child.**

It can be a powerful moment when a child learns the meaning of charity while helping to serve food at a homeless shelter, visiting the sick, or making a cake for someone who has just had a death in the family. Doing something for someone out of kindness (and not for personal reward) can be one of the most fulfilling experiences a child or an adult can have.

**Teach your foster child to practice acts of kindness and express gratitude.**

You can always tell when children are starting to do better in their own lives – they begin to say, *"Thank you, that was a good meal,"* or *"I appreciate your helping me,"* or *"I like when you encourage me."* Teach your children to carry out acts of kindness toward one another – kindnesses that are not performed to get something back in return. If children can learn skills of caring and sharing (without worrying about rewards), there is a better chance they will continue to choose positive, helpful behavior over negative, hurtful behavior.

**Encourage youth to live a spiritually balanced life.**

Prayer and other spiritual activities by themselves will not make children better. It is tying prayer to learning skills, building relationships, and developing self-discipline – all of these together make a difference. Religious home habits help create an atmosphere of warmth, an atmosphere we would like to pervade our homes. These habits include setting aside some time for reflection, for private prayer, and for reading the Holy Scriptures and other devotional books.

You might ask: *"Why can't we just develop private spirituality for our kids? Why must we participate in public worship?"*

The answer is simple and straightforward: Our children have been marginalized enough. They have been hurt. They have retreated into their own inner sanctuaries. To be human is to be part of a community that is caring and sharing – a community of worship. We should not deprive our children of this opportunity to develop a most important dimension of their lives.

Spiritual growth is an essential part of every child's life, as important as physical, emotional, social, and academic growth. Without spiritual growth, none of the other areas will mean much. Foster Parents can teach the children in their care how to build lives of faith and good moral values by modeling the importance of their own faith lives and moral behavior.

# CHAPTER 19

# Handling Transitions

*It's morning. As Robin awakens, she looks around the unfamiliar room. She slept little last night. Her mother had always warned Robin about strangers, and now she's in the midst of them. Robin hears people up and about. "What am I supposed to do?" she thinks frantically. "Lie in bed until someone comes and tells me to get up, or get dressed and go downstairs? Did anyone tell me last night? I can't remember. Where are mom and dad? I want to see them! Do they know where I am?" As these questions engulf and overwhelm Robin, she pulls the covers over her head to try and block them out.*

This account provides you with an example of what a profound, frightening, and confusing change it is for a child to move from one home to another when there is little or no chance to prepare for it. Many foster children have gone through this experience a number of times before they come to live with you. The opportunity to plan ahead and make some preparations makes a transition easier.

We've talked about the problems foster children have when they do not experience healthy attachments to their parents and how traumatic separations are for them. In this chapter, we will discuss some things that you can do to help lessen the trauma that foster children experience when they move in and out of homes.

## Preparing for Placement

There are a number of ways to prepare for the placement of a foster child in your home. Good preparation can prevent problems and make the child's transition to and stay in your home smoother.

### Get as much training as possible.

Through training, you as foster parents can:

- Learn and gain a better understanding of how children come into the system and what their issues are.

- Improve your ability to help these children become successful members of a new family and eventually return to a permanent placement.

### Identify appropriate discipline techniques and consequences.

These are necessary for managing behavioral problems and teaching the child how to live in a healthy family environment.

- Determine what kinds of consequences you can use to motivate or correct the child. (See Chapters 9-11 for a review of consequences.)
- Learn and practice the various teaching methods discussed in this book that can be used to praise the child, teach skills that he or she will need in future situations, correct misbehavior, and calm down situations where the child loses self-control.

**Know your state's licensing regulations and stay in compliance.**

Knowing and following the rules and laws that govern the placement and care of children help ensure a safe environment for youth. It also gives your home credibility as an effective place of care for young people.

**Set clear expectations.**

When a child enters your home, be sure to set clear house rules and explain predictable family events to the child. This helps to reduce fear and prevent confusion and misunderstandings. A child may come into your home with a history of physical and/or sexual abuse. Clear house rules can help protect your family and the foster child by decreasing the likelihood of inappropriate behaviors.

You can set simple house rules on the following issues and review them with a child before he or she moves into a your home:

- Meal times
- Bedroom and bathroom privacy

- Appropriate affection and boundaries
- Clothing
- Touching
- Appropriate playtime activities
- Daily routines
- Keeping secrets

By reviewing rules with a new foster child and having your own children respect the same rules, you can prevent many placement problems and keep kids safe.

## Going Home or to Another Placement

A foster home is designed to be a temporary placement. After the child and his or her family have met their goals, reunification with the family or placement in a more permanent program may occur. Regardless of whether the child goes home or to another placement, there are certain professional expectations that Foster Parents must fulfill to ensure the success of the child in his or her new home. These expectations include the following:

### Host visits between the child and parents or the new Foster Parents.

Just as preplacement meetings were arranged and successfully completed by the Foster Parent and child, the same process needs to occur as the Foster Parent helps the child move to his or her family or next placement. Foster Parents, parents, caseworker, program supervisor, and/or others set a date for the transition and how many preplacement visits should occur. Foster Parents should do everything in their power to help make the transition as smooth as possible for the child.

Clearly communicate information about the move to the child. Once the team has decided on a transition date, all of the specifics about the move must be clearly communicated to the child. This will reduce some of the child's anxiety. Change is hard for everyone! And it is especially hard if the child is moving to a new home. Imagine what it must feel like for a child who may have moved several times in his or her young life. The foster family should talk openly about the move and be available to answer any questions the child may have. Often, younger children have a hard time understanding time frames. A Foster Parent can provide a calendar to help the child see how many days are left until the transition takes place. All details should be actively and openly addressed with the child: the time of day the move will occur, who's providing transportation, opportunity to see the new home, and others. Remember: The more informed the child is, the less anxious he or she will be when the transition takes place.

### Help bring closure between the Foster Parents and the child.

It's normal for a child to have mixed emotions about a transition. On one hand, he or she is excited about returning home or going to a new home, meeting new friends or being reunited with old friends, and (usually) starting at a new school. On the other hand, with every new beginning comes an ending. The child will have to say good-bye to friends, classmates, teachers, neighbors, and the foster family. Foster Parents should play a major role in helping the foster child say his or her good-byes. Closure activities might include hosting a going away-party, bringing a video camera or still camera to school, making a scrapbook, exchanging addresses, and others. All of these activities give children "permission" to attach to other people while maintaining the bond with the friends and foster family they will leave behind.

**Help the child prepare for the move.**

As we have mentioned, moving day should be planned well in advance, if possible. Therefore, the child should have plenty of time to pack all the personal things he or she collected prior to and during the stay in the foster home. Property should be carefully packed in suitable luggage that the child can keep after he or she leaves the home. In addition, the foster child should take pictures and other memorabilia to his or her new home. Once again, these serve as connections back to the foster home.

**Recognize the attachment between Foster Parents and the child.**

Even if the transition is a successful and happy one, it is normal for Foster Parents to be sad and feel a sense of loss. You have invested your time, heart, and home in your foster child, and, because of the good work you have done, the child and his or her family have been able to achieve the goals that were established. Give yourself and your foster child permission to grieve, and set aside time for you and your foster child to discuss these feelings.

### Encourage contact between the child and Foster Parents after the child moves.

Once the transition is complete, it is important for the family or new foster family to feel comfortable about calling you for advice and suggestions in dealing with the child. In the most successful transitions, the frequency and type of contact is discussed prior to the child's moving. You can be a valuable information source to the family or new foster family because you have insight into what motivates the child, what he or she likes and dislikes, and which teaching techniques the child responds to best. The family or new foster family should be encouraged to support the child's decision to write, call, or visit you. This must be decided on a case-by-case basis, taking into account the best interests of the child.

### Provide notice.

Occasionally, Foster Parents decide that they can no longer provide a home for a specific child or that they can no longer continue to be Foster Parents. As a general rule, Foster Parents should provide a 30-day notice so that a new home and a successful transition plan can be put into place.

## Summary

Although the "real world" is not perfect, it is beneficial to set goals that will help foster children successfully manage transitions. Frequently moving from one placement to another can be a traumatic event for foster children. When a child's concerns are addressed before the move, he or she will probably be less upset, anxious, and frightened. The information presented in this chapter can empower you as foster parents to be more involved in crucial decisions and help make the placement of a child in your home a positive and lasting experience.

# References

Annie E. Casey Foundation, **Family to Family: Tools for Rebuilding Foster Care.** (Online). Available: http://www.aecf.org/familytofamily/

Bayless, L., & Love, L. (Eds.) (1990). **Assessing Attachment, Separation and Loss.** Atlanta, GA: Child Welfare Institute.

Cartledge, G., & Milburn, J.F. (Eds.) (1980). **Teaching Social Skills to Children.** New York: Pergamon Press.

Combs, M.L., & Slaby, D.A. (1977). Social skills training with children. In B.B. Lahey & A.E. Kazdin (Eds.), **Advances in Clinical Child Psychology** (pp. 161-201). New York: Plenum Press.

Covey, S.R. (1997). **The 7 Habits of Highly Effective Families.** New York: Golden Books

Dowd, T., & Tierney, J. (1992). **Teaching Social Skills to Youth.** Boys Town, NE: Boys Town Press

Fahlberg, V. (1991). **A Child's Journey through Placement**. Indianapolis, IN: Perspectives Press.

Gresham, F.M. (1981). Assessment of children's social skills. **Journal of School Psychology,** 19(2), 120-133.

Klaus, M.H., & Kennell, J.H. (1976). **Maternal-Infant Bonding.** St. Louis, MO: C.V. Mosby Company.

Mott, M.A., Authier, K., Shannon, K.K., Arneil, J.M., & Daly, D. (1995). **Treatment Foster Family Services: Development, Implementation, and Outcome of a National Multi-site Program.** Unpublished manuscript.

**New World College Dictionary.** (1997). New York, NY: Simon & Schuster, Inc.

Patterson, G.R., Dishion, T.J., & Bank, L. (1984). Family interaction: A process model of deviancy training. **Aggressive Behavior,** 10, 253-267.

Steinberg, Z., & Knitzer, J. (1992). Classrooms for emotionally and behaviorally disturbed students: Facing the challenge. **Behavioral Disorders,** 17(2), 145-156.

Stephens, T.M. (1978). **Social Skills in the Classroom.** Columbus, OH: Ohio State University.

Sue, D., & Sue, D.W. (1990). **Counseling the Culturally Different.** New York: John Wiley and Sons, Inc.

# Index

| Cover Design: | Margie Utesch |
| Page Layout: | Anne Hughes |
| Production: | Mary Steiner |